THE HOUSE WITH THE BROKEN TWO

The House with the Broken Two

~ *a birthmother remembers* ~

MYRL COULTER

ANVIL PRESS | VANCOUVER | 2011

Anvil Press Publishers Inc.
P.O. Box 3008, Main Post Office
Vancouver, B.C. V6B 3X5 Canada
www.anvilpress.com

LIBRARY AND ARCHIVES CANADA CATALOGUING IN PUBLICATION

Coulter, Myrl
     The house with the broken two : a birthmother remembers
/ Myrl Coulter.

ISBN 978-1-897535-72-1

     1. Coulter, Myrl. 2. Birthmothers—Canada—Biography.
3. Adoption—Social aspects—Canada. I. Title.

HV874.82.C69A3 2011   362.82'98092   C2011-901551-X

Printed and bound in Canada
Cover design by Mutasis Creative
Interior design by HeimatHouse

Represented in Canada by the Literary Press Group
Distributed by the University of Toronto Press

The publisher gratefully acknowledges the financial assistance of the Canada Council for the Arts, the Canada Book Fund, and the Province of British Columbia through the B.C. Arts Council and the Book Publishing Tax Credit.

For my family

ACKNOWLEDGMENTS

A number of resources were very helpful to me as I wrote this book. Of these, among the most important were *Gone to an Aunt's* by Ann Petrie; *The Girls Who Went Away* by Ann Fessler; *Finding Families, Finding Ourselves: English Canada Encounters Adoption from the Nineteenth Century to the 1990s* by Veronica Strong-Boag; and *Ten Thousand Roses: The Making of a Feminist Revolution* by Judy Rebick.

I want to express my deep gratitude to the following people:

—The Writers Studio at Simon Fraser University, especially Betsy Warland, for organizing the 2010 First Book Competition.

—John Mavin, for one of the best phone calls I've ever received.

—Karen Connelly, for choosing my manuscript.

—Brian Kaufman and everyone at Anvil Press.

—Aimee Ouellette, for wise editorial insights.

—Janice Williamson, for unwavering support.

—Andrea O'Reilly, for everything she has ever written and her dedication to all mothers everywhere.

—my mother, who would not like this book, but who would probably speak to me again eventually, if only she could.

—my father, who would be proud.

—my sisters and my brother, who understand the way no one else can.

—my four adult children, who fill my life with hope.

—my husband, who made it possible for me to write.

CONTENTS

Writing from Memory

MEMORY IS SLIPPERY. Fuzzy one minute, starkly vivid the next, memory operates as if it has its own will, emphasizing the highlights of a life even as it simultaneously diminishes less desirable, harsher moments. Memories of an event last much longer than the event itself. Essentially, once a moment has passed, all that remains of that moment is memory. And while an actual event becomes a memory, the memory of it becomes the event. Supported only by remaining artifacts, such as ticket stubs or photographs, memories of past events exist largely in the invisible realms of abiding emotions and enduring sensory remnants, in those ineffable places where the various truths of that event live on.

In this book, I recreate moments from different phases of my life as a series of related narratives. These selected moments don't exist in isolation from other life moments that I do not include here. Sifting through my memories, I had to decide which ones connected directly or indirectly to two life-changing events: surrendering my first-born child to the closed adoption system back in 1968 and welcoming him back into my life thirty-six years later.

Siphoned out of recollections stored somewhere in my psyche, this book is memoir, not autobiography: not a complete telling from the beginning of my life to the present, but an exploration of what I now see as related family histories and events from before, during, and after the adoption. Linking a series of memories together to create a cohesive story has been an exhilarating and daunting exercise. I started the project because I wanted my son to know the family he should have always been part of. As I proceeded, I experienced a new version of me, one who now understands the multi-faceted answers to a question I had long avoided asking myself: How could I possibly have given away my first child?

Some memories, even the ones very far in my past, are still astonishingly present to me, vibrantly etched as if on a pane of glass in my mind. Those moments flowed easily onto my pages. Other memories, even some that are relatively recent, are much murkier. I reimagined those delicately, filling in details I didn't quite remember such as the time of day, what I would have been wearing, what songs may have been playing on the radio, what words filled the conversations.

I aimed for accuracy when locating my experiences, and those of my family, in the social and cultural contexts of my municipal, national, and international communities. In doing so, I often felt like a detective, researching the past to frame the progress of my life. Many times my research uncovered historical nuggets that brought memories long-submerged floating to the surface of my mind: the Winnipeg flood of 1966, the smell of the St. Boniface Cathedral on fire, the words of Randy Bachman's haunting song "Undun" resonating in my head. I used those recovered memory fragments to put muscle, sinew, and flesh on the bones of my stories. This is what literary memoir does: create again, as true to the moment as possible according to the resources available to the writer.

Why tell this very personal story? A number of reasons come to mind. The obvious one is because of its relevance to the complicated history of adoption in North America. The closed adoption process that was predominant from the end of World War II until the late 1970s affected, and continues to affect, thousands and thousands of North Americans, whether they are from birth families or adoptive families. Moreover, I wanted to explore how an ordinary family like mine, a family who celebrated the arrival of each and every child, could have let one of their own go, supposedly never to be thought about, heard from, or spoken of again. My personal perspective deepened as I realized that many, many families had and have hidden stories like this, stories that usually remain untold.

Perhaps the most important function of memoir is that it connects people. In this era of instant communication, technological hookups, capitalism in crisis, economic pandemonium, environmental turbulence, and frenetic cultural upheaval in general, we need each other's stories more than ever. I wrote this book because I want people to know this story, because I believe that knowing each other's stories turns strangers into neighbours. To motivate ourselves to work toward a better world, we must understand each other's stories.

While recording my memories, I often reminded myself that this is my story, not anyone else's. It is my perspective alone. I know that two or three people involved in the same event will have two or three or even more different versions of that event and its consequences. That doesn't make any one of them false, just differently experienced, differently remembered. I have included some events where I wasn't present but felt they were relevant to the overall narrative. They were told to me by others, and I wrote them as I heard them.

As I wrote, my goal was to treat everyone involved in my story with respect and dignity while staying true to my memory of each moment as it happened to me. I thank members of my extended family for helping me retrieve details from long ago as accurately as possible. Nevertheless, I take full responsibility for what I have written and any mistakes I may have made.

CHAPTER ONE

The Edict

THIS MEMORY IS FROM a time in my life that was so long ago it feels as if it belongs to someone else, but I know that it's mine.

*** *** ***

Sitting up in her hospital bed, a worn blanket covering her legs, the eighteen-year-old spread out her hands to show her mother. All the nails extended just beyond the tips of her fingers, each one manicured and polished a soft coral pink with no hints of hangnails or chewed ragged edges visible anywhere.

"One good thing from all this, Mom. My nails have never looked better."

Her mother nodded and managed a small smile.

"Of course, I've done them every day, ever since I had to quit working. I've never spent any time on my nails before. I usually just ignored them, so they were always broken. It never seemed worth the effort to polish them, but I've always wanted beautiful nails like yours. So when I found instructions on how to have gorgeous hands in one of my *Seventeen* magazines, I followed them to the letter, every day for the past four months. And it worked. Don't they look great? Mom?"

Her mother nodded again, then sighed as she looked down at her own tired hands clenched in her lap. After a moment, she turned her attention back to her daughter.

"How do you feel, dear?"

"Fine, Mom. I feel great. I was a little scared, but now it's over and I can hardly wait to get home and do things again. Go to football games and see my friends at the swimming pool. Really, I'm fine, not sore a bit. Well, maybe a little, but I'll be home before you know it and I'll look good and no one will know. It'll be like I've been away on the best trip ever, just like you said. You'll see."

The girl ran out of words and breath at the same time. She waited for her mother to respond, not knowing what to expect next. She knew her mother wouldn't ask about the actual birth, and she was glad about that. She didn't want to tell her mother about that experience, about being alone in the labour room, about the glaring lights of the delivery room, about behaving badly as she succumbed to panic, about hearing disparaging comments from the nurses. No, she wasn't going to tell anyone any of that, ever.

They sat in silence for several minutes. Her mother hesitated, started to speak a few times, and finally could not resist the question.

"How is he?"

The girl beamed as she answered.

"He's excellent. They brought me this form today, a paper for the social worker that I had to sign. Right at the top there was this big space where it asked about the health of the baby at birth and guess what! The doctor wrote "EXCELLENT." In really big letters, too. The nurse said they usually just put "good." That's the regular word, but not this time. This time it was "EXCELLENT." Of course, I knew he would be excellent. I followed the food guide, took prenatal vitamins, and drank lots of milk. Ugh. I hate milk. But I even made myself drink an extra glass on the nights I was on kitchen cleanup duty at the home. Forced it right down while I was drying the dishes. That's why he's excellent. Maybe that helped my nails, too."

"I'm sure it did, dear."

The girl suddenly threw back the hospital blanket.

"I didn't show you my toenails. I did them today. They don't look as good as my fingernails do because I haven't been able to reach them for a while, but I think they look a lot better than they used to. Over the last few months, I soaked my feet a lot, especially at night when I couldn't sleep. I'd get up and tiptoe down the hall to the tub room and put towels on the floor by the door so no one could hear the water running. I didn't want to wake any of the other girls. Now that I can reach my feet again, I wanted my toes to look as good as my fingernails. So this morning, I just closed my curtain at feeding time when the other ladies have their . . . and did my toenails. Don't they look great?"

Her mother nodded. Another few minutes passed in silence. Both looked around the room for something to say. Two of the other women were sleeping, and one was reading a book. In the hallway, an orderly manoeuvred a stretcher around the nursing station, the occupant's hands cradling her belly.

Glancing back at her mother, the girl took a breath.

"I'm not supposed to see him. They said it would be better."

"Yes. I think that's for the best. When do you sign the adoption papers?"

"I'm not sure. I think I have to sign something before I leave the hospital."

Her mother nodded but said nothing.

"How's Dad? Does he know I'm coming home soon?"

"Yes. He knows."

The girl fell silent. Her mother sighed again before she spoke.

"Your father wishes never to speak of this again."

This time it was the girl who looked down at her hands.

After her mother left, the girl sat on her bed watching the daily routine of the ward. Nurses and doctors strode in and out of the big room, tending to the other mothers' concerns, giving detailed answers to their questions. They didn't stop at her bed, and she didn't call them over. She didn't think she had any particular concerns and had learned not to ask the questions that floated around inside her head. She remembered asking her family doctor last summer if birth control pills were available in Canada yet. She hadn't planned on asking that question; it just blurted out of her mouth. The doctor had looked at her sternly and said that if she asked a question like that again, he'd have to call her mother.

Just before dinnertime, her boyfriend arrived. He had visited her often at the home, but she hadn't seen him for a while. They talked awkwardly about nothing for a few minutes. Soon they decided to go for a walk up and down the hallways. After a few laps around the ward, she guided him to a nursery window, where she stopped and pointed to the third bassinet from the left. Standing side by side, they gazed at their sleeping baby in silence for a few moments. Then, without looking at her, he said, "I gotta go," and walked away.

At feeding time that evening, she closed the curtains around her bed and picked up the new *Seventeen* magazine her mother had brought her. Trust Mom to bring last month's issue, she thought as she noticed the date in the top corner: April 1968. Even though she had already read it, she flipped through the pages again. This time the articles seemed to mock her life: "They Don't Tell You Everything in Biology Class." No kidding, she thought. "Ways to Calm Our Parents' Fears." Not possible, she figured. "How to Say No to a Friend." What about a boyfriend? she wondered. "Be a Party-Smarty." She couldn't remember the last party she went to. Playing with the ends of her long, blond hair and pausing to admire her fingernails every few minutes, she scanned through the rest of the pages. Soon the magazine slid off the bed to the floor.

Darkness blanketed the room when she woke up. Pale yellow hallway lights shone through a crack in the door. The air was dry, oozing with the surprising silence that can come over a large institution in the middle of the night. Even the voices over the public address system spoke softly, whispering their messages in muted, measured tones. Without checking the clock, she knew what time it was. She had woken up the last two nights at exactly the same time.

She got out of bed, slipped her coral-pink toenails into her slippers, and reached for her dressing gown. Red with quilted heart-shaped pockets, it had a scalloped hemline and big puffy sleeves, each with a small white bow at the wrist. Her parents had given it to her for Christmas two years ago. She remembered her mother saying that her father had picked it out: her mother said she thought the hearts and bows were too fussy, but her father insisted on buying it. The girl had worn it every morning and night since the day she got it.

Quietly, she slipped out the door and down the hall. Soon her hands and forehead leaned against the glass of the nursery window as she watched him lie in his bassinet. His eyes were open. She hadn't seen him with open eyes before. The first night he had been sleeping. Last night he was crying so hard that his eyes were squeezed shut. Tonight, he was wide awake and calm, gazing around, not seeing anything, slightly moving his head back and forth a little bit: not fussing, just looking.

Usually staffed by two, the nursery seemed to have only one nurse on duty tonight. The girl hadn't seen this one before. This nurse had a round, friendly face and almost smiled as she glanced up at the window. The other nurses never even acknowledged the girl's presence; they simply ignored her as if she were an ineffective ghost who would eventually just drift off into the darkness. Sometimes the nurses whispered back and forth to each other, nodding almost imperceptibly toward the window without looking directly at it. Maybe they thought the girl didn't see what they thought of her, but she did.

This nurse was different. She glanced up at the window several times, as if she wanted to say something. Thinking she was going to be asked to leave, the girl started to back away but almost immediately changed her mind. No one can stop me from looking at him, she thought. She glanced up and down the hall. It was deserted. She turned back to the nursery, once again feeling the cool smoothness of the glass against her forehead. After a moment or two, she heard the door to the nursery crack open. The young nurse leaned out into the hall.

"I'm not supposed to do this, but . . . would you like to hold him? Come quickly. I'll get you a gown. You can sit here."

Gingerly, she settled him into the crook of her arm. At first she was afraid to breathe, but soon she relaxed. He felt so light and warm. His little chest rose and fell rhythmically. She ran her hand over his legs as they shifted gently inside the blue blanket. She fondled both his feet until she had counted each tiny toe. She could see his heart beating in the soft spot on the top of his head. She bent her head closer to inhale his fresh baby smell, then stroked his cheek with her index finger. He seemed to have a need to be held, a need matched by hers to hold. He didn't make a sound, just looked around: looking, looking, looking. He truly was excellent, she thought. One little hand escaped the blanket, one little hand with its tiny fingers fisted over his thumb. She put her index finger under his fist, just like she had done with her baby sister, and his fingers curled around it instantly. They sat there just like that, the two of them: him hanging on and her hanging on. One moment branded on one heart for a lifetime. All too soon, the nurse tapped her on the shoulder.

"You can't stay any longer. I'll take him now."

Outside the nursery door, she took a deep breath and forced

herself to move forward, one foot after the other. Holding her back straight, she made herself walk tall. She knew she had good posture. She knew that the secret to walking tall was to pretend that someone was about to kick her in the butt at the same time that someone else was going to punch her in the stomach. Her uncle had told her that. She hadn't seen her uncle in a very long time.

Back in her room, she fumbled in her little cosmetic bag for a nail file. Using the light leaking in from the hallway, she filed and filed until her fingernails were reduced to nothing. She pulled out her nail polish remover and scrubbed off all the coral pink. The fumes made her want to cry, but she didn't. She wouldn't. In the last nine months, she hadn't cried once. Crying would make it real. Swallowing hard, she drenched a fresh tissue with polish remover and reached for her toes.

CHAPTER TWO

In the Beginning

MY FEISTY PATERNAL GRANDMOTHER was always very present in my life. I wear her name: Myrl. The spelling of our name is an Irish version of the androgynous and, in my estimation, decidedly unattractive *Merle*. People usually have difficulty with my name because Myrl is a weird-looking word. They don't know how to say it (it rhymes with *girl*), much less spell it.

I have been accused of having a name with no vowel in it. When I hear this, I point to the *y* and recite the old vowel adage, "a, e, i, o, u, and sometimes *y*." I am the sometimes *y*. During my teenage years, I had a testy, ambivalent relationship with my name: I liked it because it was different, and I disliked it because it was too different. For a while, I even considered switching to my middle name, because being Louise would make things easier for me. But I didn't know how I would explain that to my very-much-alive grandmother Myrl, so I soon abandoned that idea.

After years of resisting it, I've finally made friends with my name. But even when I disliked it the most, I always liked, and still do, that I was named for my grandmother. Curiously, it wasn't until the end of her life that I realized people had actually called her by our name. She was always Granny to me. Many years later, listening to the minister speak during her funeral service, I was startled each time he called her Myrl, thinking that he was suddenly talking to me.

My family's roots are firmly Canadian, more specifically Western Canadian. I'm not even the second or third generation from immigration, but the fourth: my grandparents' grandparents were the newcomers to this country. Nevertheless, in Canada, ancestral roots remain strong for a long time, and my family is no exception. As a child growing up in Winnipeg, I somehow felt that I was only steps away from being Scottish, even though my four grandparents provided a strong blend of Irish and Icelandic heritage as well.

My mother's father was a tall, dark-haired man with a terrific smile and a deep voice. At least I remember him as tall, but that could be because I wasn't. He owned a car dealership in Winnipeg. My mother often told me how she learned to drive at a young age and always had her own car. I was envious. Her father was also an avid horse-racing fan, a passion that he passed on to my uncle who went on to become the founder of Winnipeg's Assiniboia Downs racetrack. I liked that my uncle owned a racetrack. I was the only one of my high school friends who had access to a season pass. I only used it once, but it was memorable. A horse named Merle's Pride was a long shot that day. I didn't bet on it because I didn't like the spelling of its name. The horse came from the back of the pack and finished first. When I saw my uncle, he asked me how much I had won. I had to tell him I hadn't placed a bet. He shook his head and smiled at me: "I did. Just because of that name."

My maternal grandfather spent every winter in Florida, so I only saw him during the summertime, although I know I went to Florida once to visit him. I don't remember that visit. It exists in old black-and-white photos of me as a smiling toddler in a sunsuit with an oversized bonnet on her head and a golf club in her hands. It's a real golf club, not a toy. I can almost see my mother standing just out of camera range, close by in case I bonk myself on the head. I think my grandfather and my great-grandfather are also nearby. In my mental image my great-grandfather is very tall and has white hair, but I can't really see him. I only know what he looked like because of the pictures I've seen of him.

Dating this memory from family records, I know that when my mother and I went to Florida, I was about two-and-a-half-years old. I have no actual memory of playing with that golf club while three generations of my family watched and took pictures. I've created that memory out of those old black-and-white photographs and words I've heard spoken around me by older generations, words I may not have paid any attention to at the time, but words I heard nonetheless. Both the photos and the words have seeded themselves in my psyche as my first memory, a constructed narrative I learned from my family and its archives.

The year I was fourteen, my maternal grandfather returned from his winter sojourn in Florida later than usual. I don't know why. I do know that he came to visit my mother one sunny June afternoon so that he could meet my baby sister, his newest grandchild. I remember being disappointed that he left before I got home from school. A few nights later, he had massive heart failure and died in his sleep. I can still picture him and I can almost hear his voice. I wish I could remember his funeral, but my siblings and I didn't go to his service because my uncle said that funerals were no place for children. What I remember most vividly about that day is the anguished look on my mother's face as she left our house for the church.

My mother had lost her own mother years earlier. My Icelandic grandmother died young, before I was born, when my mother was only seventeen years old. My middle name, Louise, is an anglicized version of her Icelandic one, Lovisa. She is my missing grandmother, the absent ancestor who regularly haunts my thoughts. I have an old black-and-white photo of her that I look at often. Wearing capri pants, white ankle socks, and high heels, she sits smiling on the bumper of a car. Charming as it is, the photograph does not reveal enough for me, giving no sense of what her voice sounded like or what words she would have said to me. My mother told me that my grandmother was petite, very talented with a sewing needle, and that everyone who knew her loved her, especially my grandfather, who called her Lou and was highly protective of her because she had had rheumatic fever as a child and was consequently always a little frail, but apparently not too frail to give birth to four children.

On the other side of my family, my father's father was deeply attached to his roots in Scotland, so his heritage was the most visible one to me. Although proudly Canadian, "reverse immigration" had reinforced his Scottishness: during World War II, my father's sister met a handsome Scot, an RAF pilot who was in Canada for training at the air base in Gimli, Manitoba. They married and she moved to Scotland for the rest of her life. A family joke is that, over the years, my aunt who was born Canadian became more Scottish than many Scots.

My paternal grandfather was a very accomplished and refined man. Born in Portage La Prairie, he was the younger of two brothers. Because their father died shortly after my grandfather was born, he and his big brother grew up strongly influenced by their own grandfather, a rugged and sternly religious Scottish Highlander. As a young man, my grandfather's brother went off to fight in World War I. Although badly gassed, he survived the war itself, but he didn't survive the flu epidemic that immediately followed it. I think my grandfather felt the loss of his brother deeply for the rest of his life. When my father was born, he was given my great-uncle's name.

Involved in the grain industry at a young age, Gramp worked his way up and was eventually appointed chief commissioner of the Canadian Wheat Board, a position he held for more than two decades. As a child, I was often told (I don't remember by whom) that my grandfather had received medals for his work in food relief during World War II: one was from England, the Cross of St. Michael and St. George, and the other was from the king of Belgium. As a child, I could recite those words, but I didn't know the significance of those medals. I didn't even know where Belgium was, much less whether or not it had a king. (It does.) I just knew that my grandfather was important beyond the scope of our family in Winnipeg. He travelled extensively, had connections all over the world, and met famous people.

For me, spending time with my paternal grandfather was much like going to history class. Gramp loved nothing more than to tell stories about his experiences to anyone who would listen. As the eldest of his Canadian grandchildren, I knew that my job was to sit quietly as he talked. Although I tried to do that most of the time, even when I was sitting quietly I couldn't have been listening very well because, no matter how hard I try, I can't remember most of the details in his stories. I remember that he talked about taking a train across Outer Mongolia. I remember that he talked about zigzagging across the Atlantic in a ship during wartime. I remember that he talked about meeting Winston Churchill. Other, less iconic names escaped me at the time and elude me still. I do remember that he talked a lot about his good friend Mike and a "Mr. Howe." I don't remember how old I was when I realized that Mr. Howe was C. D. Howe, then Canada's minister of trade and commerce, and Mike was Lester B. Pearson, Canada's fourteenth prime minister.

I'm not sure I ever saw my two grandfathers together, but I somehow have the sense that they had respect for one another. I know that during family visits one grandfather always asked my parents how the other was doing. Going through a messy file of family archives recently, I made a fascinating discovery: two of my great-great-grandfathers, one on my mother's side and one on my father's side, were born on the Isle of Lewis in Scotland, just a few years apart. From there, they both came to Canada to work for the Hudson's Bay Company. Once here, they were both invited to be part of a Franklin Expedition search party led by the Scottish explorer Dr. John Rae back in the 1850s. This discovery immediately filled my mind with images of my two ancestors shivering together on frigid windswept decks or trudging side by side across vast frozen landscapes, probably uncertain of their chances of survival, unaware that not only would they survive, but also the families they would go on to have would be joined together almost a century later.

As a child I went to visit my paternal grandparents eagerly. Their quiet home was a welcome relief from our house, a place that, to me, often felt overrun by my younger siblings. To my young eyes, Granny and Gramp lived in an oasis of calm, surrounded by the fruits of their comfortable life together, watched over by art treasures and tokens gathered from around the world. My grandfather always seemed to be off on important, mysterious (at least to me) missions that took him to exotic locations. Although Granny accompanied him at times, more often she was left behind to wait patiently for his return. I loved to watch her roam through her house, distracted but deliberate as she sought out some new old keepsake she wanted me to see. She had a slightly pitched kind of walk all her own, full of purpose, yet always ready to meander off in a new direction. My childhood memories of time I spent with Granny come back in sporadic flashes.

I remember that Granny always held my hand as we talked or walked around the house or some small garden, guiding me to follow her lead.

I remember that she once put me to sleep on an old velvet chaise longue when I stayed overnight at her house one weekend. The next day, I told my mother that Granny made me sleep in a chair. That chaise longue is still in our family, in the basement of my daughter's house. I think cats sleep on it now.

I remember that she used to watch from the sidelines as my grandfather and I skated together to the sounds of *The Blue Danube* at a downtown Winnipeg rink. She pointed us out to everyone who walked by.

She drove a green Nash Rambler that had no radio. My grandmother was always a little deaf, so my grandfather didn't see any sense in spending the extra money for a radio in her car. One day, when I was about eight or nine, I was riding in the passenger seat, long before cars had things like seat belts and child-safe door locks. I tried to roll down the window but opened the car door by mistake. With surprising swiftness and strength, Granny grabbed my arm as she slowed the car and steered it to the side of the road. Then she calmly closed the door, adjusted the window, and took a deep breath before we carried on our way. I never told my parents about that incident, and I don't think Granny did either.

When their children had grown up and were off pursuing their own lives, my grandparents sold their Winnipeg home. After that, they lived in a series of tasteful rented dwellings. Yet, no matter where they lived, their homes always looked similar. Whether it was an elegant brick duplex in Winnipeg, the spacious second floor of a classic old home in Montreal, or a light-filled apartment with a view of the Elbow River in Calgary, I knew that *Big Chief*, a large Nicholas de Grandmaison portrait of a magnificent Indian man, would always have a prominent spot on the living room wall, keeping a careful eye on all occupants from above the sofa, his amazing face a magnet to anyone who entered his domain. Under that stern gaze, my siblings and I could not misbehave, at least not outrageously. His eyes seemed to follow every move we made.

The dining room was Lotso's territory. Posed in lotus position atop the mahogany sideboard, Lotso was cast in silver, forever frozen in permanent meditation. To me, he ensured the safety of the household by sending his serene aura throughout the rooms. In one hand, he held three silver orbs, their triple gleam outshone only by the smooth patina of his perfectly round head. I don't know where he came from. I'm sure I was told many times, but I probably wasn't listening. I do know that I couldn't walk by Lotso without reaching up to touch him, perhaps imitating my grandmother who patted his head every time she meandered past his perch. To me, he was her companion. When my grandfather was away, she was never alone because Lotso was always there.

Big Chief and Lotso were just the most prominent of the treasures my grandfather acquired during his long business and diplomatic career. Silver candlesticks, engraved trays, crystal candy dishes, framed scenes from his beloved Scotland: all filled the spaces of their world. Although Granny had great affinity for them, she was also eager to share the smaller ones with her grandchildren. In fact, as I grew older, I learned not to admire anything too much because Granny would insist that I have it.

Several years after I was married, she caught me gazing at an orange ginger jar I had secretly coveted for years. That day, it left with me as I made the three-hour drive back home to my husband and children. Within three months, the ginger jar lay shattered on my bedroom floor. Not realizing its significance, my husband had used it to prop open a window on a particularly blustery spring day while I was out grocery shopping. As I gathered up the pieces, I felt as shattered as that ginger jar and could never bring myself to tell Granny that it had been destroyed under my watch. Unfortunately, it wasn't difficult to keep my secret because neither she nor my grandfather ever visited my home.

CHAPTER THREE

Baby Boom

EXCEPT FOR A THREE-YEAR GAP, I grew up in Winnipeg, the city I was born in, the city my mother was born in. When I was not yet a year old, in the spring of 1950, Winnipeg had a big flood. Situated on the flat prairie, on a flood plain at the junction of the Red and Assiniboine Rivers, Winnipeg is not unfamiliar with being flooded. The 1950 flood, however, must have felt biblical in scope: a flood of floods, *the* flood in a series of many. Early in May that year, within the span of a few days, Winnipeggers went from being blasé about rising waters to anxiously watching the river every moment, to becoming refugees in flight from their normally placid metropolis. Staid, tranquil Winnipeg turned from a small prairie city into a large prairie lake. Automobile traffic disappeared as city streets transformed into waterways filled with boats of all sizes, each helping with the greatest mass evacuation ever undertaken in Canada to that point.

Neighbourhoods that usually stayed dry during flood times—such as St. Vital, Fort Garry, and Norwood (where my mother grew up)—succumbed to the Red River's murky waters as dikes failed one after another. I don't know exactly where my parents and I lived at that time, but I think I'm safe in assuming it was in the Norwood area. I do know that we lived on the top floor of a house owned by a friendly older couple who lived on the first floor of the same house. My mother and I were among the over one-hundred-thousand people evacuated from Winnipeg that year. She took me to Lethbridge, where we stayed with my father's aunt until it was safe to come home.

The flood I lived through but can't remember pulls on me to learn more about it. Most of the evacuees were women and children. Many men stayed behind to work with the army rescuing people who may have been trapped by the rising waters. Fortunately, although losses were massive, most of the flood damage was to property. One fatality occurred when a man named Lawson Ogg went down to his basement to repair a pump just before floodwaters deluged his house. My father, my uncles, and probably both of my grandfathers were in that flood-fighting group of civilian men who stayed behind. To this day, whenever I come across archival pictures and film clips about the 1950 flood, I find myself scanning the scenes for familiar faces.

Two years after the big flood, in the summer that I turned three, my parents moved us to Moncton, New Brunswick. I'm not exactly sure why. In retrospect, it seems like a very unusual move for my parents to have made, because both their extended families were firmly planted in Winnipeg. Over the years, the only thing I can remember my parents saying about that move is that my father took a job with a finance company and they transferred him to a branch office in the Maritimes. I don't remember what the name of the company was, just that it consisted of initials, not words. Moving under the surface of the official family story, I suspect that my parents may have wanted the adventure of a move, the experience of taking themselves and their small family away from the familiarity of home to someplace new where they could establish themselves independently, away from parental and sibling eyes.

We were a baby boom family in action. During the three years we spent in Moncton, our small family doubled in size. I know that my mother was already pregnant with my brother when we headed east, so he was conceived in Winnipeg but born in Moncton. My middle sister was conceived and born in Moncton. My next sister was conceived in Moncton but born shortly after we moved back to Winnipeg, the summer that I turned six. My youngest sister, who came along eight years later, missed the Moncton experience entirely. She smiles patiently whenever the rest of us talk about it. Not that we have much to say. As the oldest, even I have only a few distinct memories of Moncton.

I know that we lived in a little house situated at a T-junction. My bedroom was at the front of the house. Several times a night, my room filled with the bright glow of car headlights for several moments until darkness took over again as the traffic veered off. I can't confirm this memory because I have no outside pictures of that house and my mother says I always slept soundly as a child.

Moncton is where television came into our lives. We were the only family on our street to have one. In those early days of television broadcasting, programs didn't come on until four o'clock in the afternoon. My mother would turn the screen on about fifteen minutes early to warm it up. As we waited, we watched the test pattern with its strange markings in the corners of the screen and the profiled head of a native man in the middle. I liked the test pattern—I liked its stillness. The most vivid memory I have of our time in Moncton is of the day we began our move back west. The house was chaos as my father loaded our suitcases into the car. I was supposed to be watching my brother while my mother gave directions to the moving men as they packed our furniture into a big truck. It was a beautiful, sunny day, so my baby sister was sitting quietly in her playpen on the lawn. Leaving the movers to finish up, we got into our car and drove down the street, my brother and I leaning up against the back seat looking through the window at our receding house. Suddenly my mother gasped: "The baby! We forgot the baby." My father turned the car around immediately. When we got back to the house, the moving men were standing around her playpen. "We were just trying to figure out how to pack her," one of them said. My mother retrieved my sister, and the moving men put the playpen in the truck.

I always thought that was a funny story. I used to tell it often at family gatherings, used to like how it made everyone burst into big belly laughs. Then one year, my sister told me how much she hated that story, hated the idea that she was almost left behind. I felt badly and never told it again. Well, until now.

Just as I'm not sure exactly why we moved to Moncton, I'm not sure exactly why we moved back to Winnipeg. Since neither of my parents will ever be able to elaborate on their reasons now, my mind turns to speculation: perhaps established family ties pulled too strongly for them to resist any longer, or perhaps their young family was growing so much that they decided they needed to be closer to extended family members, or perhaps things didn't work out for my father in his work down there, or perhaps as Western Canadians they just couldn't wrap their heads around living in Eastern Canada for the rest of their lives. Back in the 1950s, there was even more distance between the East and West in Canada than there is now.

Some years ago, my mother briefly opened up a little bit about the end of our family's sojourn in Moncton. She told me that one of my uncles, her oldest brother, had offered my father a job at his company in Winnipeg so they decided to move back. Once there, the promised job disappeared, and a permanent family rift began. As far as I know, my father and that uncle never talked to each other again. Despite my urging, my mother was reluctant to say anything further, and I was never able to substantiate this story with either my father or my uncle, so speculation will have to fill this gap in my version of our family history.

We travelled back to Winnipeg just as we had travelled to Moncton: by train. I have no memory of the journey to Moncton, but I do have vague flashes of the journey back to Winnipeg. Like his family, my father had grown heavier while we were in the east, so he was not a small man at this point in his life. My mother was very pregnant, so she was not small either. Travelling from Moncton to Winnipeg is a long way by train, so we had to live and sleep in our compartment for several days and nights. But train compartments are compact, and my parents weren't. They had more than a little difficulty chasing after two children who could dart out the compartment door and immediately disappear down the corridor. My mother told me she had to keep ringing the bell to ask the conductor to fetch my brother or me. At just over a year old, my little sister was somewhat easier to manage: at least one of my parents could still move fast enough to catch her.

Back in Winnipeg, I'm not sure what came first: my newest baby sister or the house that we would live in for the next fifteen years. What I do know for certain is that my mother did not go into labour during the train trip, that it was one of the hottest summers on record (I haven't checked the official record—that's just what the family story says), that we moved into a tidy one-and-a-half-storey house with a yard full of oak trees, and that I started Grade One that September.

Chapter Four

The House with the Broken Two

TWO OF MY SISTERS and I stood in front of our old Winnipeg house. We gazed in silence for a few moments.

"My god, it's so little. How did we all fit in there?"

"It looks a little rundown. Kind of sad, somehow."

My middle sister, who has always been a far better observer of detail than I, pointed at the front door. "Look at that," she said. "The two in the house number is still broken."

None of us had lived in Winnipeg for a long time: almost thirty years. We didn't even visit Winnipeg much anymore now that all our aunts and uncles had moved on from this earth. But it was spring, and our old high school was having a reunion. I had graduated from that school, and three of my siblings had started their high school years there, so we were back in our old hometown.

The house with the broken two was still white, but all the window trims were now a dingy dark brown. When we lived there, my parents painted the front steps and the garage doors bright red.

I liked that because it was easy to tell my friends how to find our house: "Just come to the one with the red steps." I always thought it looked like a happy house, festive, like Christmas all year round. It didn't look Christmasy anymore.

We three sisters stood staring at our old house for several minutes. I could see through the big picture window where our dining-room table used to be. I knew that beyond that was the living room and the matching rear window that looked out onto the backyard. Although the front steps were no longer red, I could still see myself sitting on them, preparing for any one of my favourite sidewalk games: hopscotch, Mother, may I, or Simon Says. On the other side of the steps was the small window to a bedroom that started out as my parents' room, but eventually became the room two of my sisters shared, not always harmoniously. I knew that beside it was the little kitchen we spent so much time in. I could picture our old table and chairs, and the pink wallboard my father put up because he got a good deal on it from a friend. I remembered my father sitting at the table in that kitchen saying that the reason he bought the house was because it was the only one he could find that had two full bathrooms. My father was in many ways a practical man.

My sisters and I could have stood there longer, but we grew concerned that anyone viewing us from the inside might think we were plotting no good, so we moved on to take a walk through our old neighbourhood. What struck me the most was that thirty years had passed and not much had changed. The fire station was still next to the police station, and the police station was still next to the library. The football field still spread out between the small grandstands on either side. The outdoor swimming pool where we all learned to swim waited for water to fill it. Even empty, it looked much the same as it did the last time I dove into it. The community centre where we skated in the winter was still at the far end of the football field. With its shiny, new clubhouse, it looked quite different, but the rinks were still in the same place. In many ways, my old neighbourhood seemed frozen in time. Only the newer model cars on the streets indicated the decades that had passed.

My sisters and I decided to walk to all our old schools. As the adult me walked the still-familiar routes, I thought how arduous those walks seemed to the child I used to be. From my first day in Grade One, I walked to school and back twice a day, coming home every noon hour for lunch. Because I was the first one in our family to go to school, and because my mother was always busy with the younger ones, I remember walking it alone. To my short little six-year-old legs, it felt like a very long way. Since becoming a mother myself, I had often remarked to my own children about how far I had to trek to get to my elementary school. Three decades later, I realized that it's not far at all: just a few blocks. Even at a slow pace, stopping to comment on the families that used to live in the houses we passed, my sisters and I covered the distance in no time.

By the time I moved to junior high school, which was located not far from my elementary school, my walks were no longer lonely. I had many friends to meet up with along the way. When I moved on to high school, my daily walk became much shorter. All I had to do was run out the back door of our house and across the football field. Getting there was easy—too easy. More often than not, I was late.

My memories from the fifteen years we lived in the house with the broken two are plentiful, but they tend to crowd on top of each other in a confusing melee. Regular, everyday, ordinary moments fuse together so that I'm unsure about what happened when. It's easier to sort through my thoughts about life in that house according to the seasons that came and went every year.

＊ ＊ ＊

The basement flooded every spring. As the sun began to rise higher and hotter in the sky, melting the snowbanks and warming the frozen ground, I knew that my father would soon put a pump at the back door to empty the water out of the basement. It would stay there for a week or so. My mother kept a pair of galoshes at the bottom of the stairs to put on her feet when she had to wade over to the washer and dryer, which were fortunately perched high in a dry corner. When my father created a "rec" room and a bedroom for my brother in that basement, he built them on a raised floor to keep everything in them dry. I suppose that was easier, and perhaps cheaper, than fixing the house's foundation.

Spring also meant taking down the storm windows and putting up the screens, usually a weekend project for the whole family that involved pails and hoses. My siblings and I formed the work crew: my father was the crew boss, my mother the general supervisor. The work crew hosed the screens down. Quite often, we "accidentally" hosed each other down as well. Once we had shaken the water off the screens, we passed them up a ladder to my father, who installed them on the window frames as we watched nervously from below. I was always worried that he would fall off the ladder. Putting the screens up was a happy time because we knew summer was coming. We stored the storm windows in the garage until fall when we would go through the whole process again in reverse, which wasn't nearly as happy a project because windows are harder to clean than screens and we knew it meant that winter was on its way.

I liked having a screen. My bedroom was tiny, so my bed was right beside the window. I didn't mind because I liked feeling the cool night air waft over me while I slept. As a teenager, I also liked the benefit of being able to close my door and blow the smoke from my secret cigarette out the middle of the screen rather than through one of those little holes in the storm windows. Smoking was the ultimate cool in those days. I tried very hard to turn myself into a smoker when I was a teenager. Fortunately for me, cigarettes always made me dizzy so I failed in that endeavour.

In the summertime, I used to lie in the backyard tanning myself with baby oil. Nobody used sunscreen back then—we used suntan lotion to get as dark as possible. As hard as it is for me to believe today, sometimes I even reflected the sun's rays back onto my face with aluminum foil. But I could never stand to be out in the hot Winnipeg sun too long. Try as I might to stay still and bake myself, I would soon grab a towel, sprint across the football field, and plunge into the community swimming pool. I took all my swimming lessons at that pool, eagerly plowing through the water back and forth from one end of the pool to the other so I could pass to the next level each summer. My parents sent all their children for those swimming lessons. They wanted us to be good swimmers because every summer we went to the lake.

The best part of summer in Winnipeg was getting out of the city. Perhaps that statement is a little unfair to my old hometown, but it's true that families who had lake cottages packed up as soon as they could in the spring, usually from the long weekend in May onward. Some escaped the muggy city by driving west to Clear Lake in Riding Mountain National Park. Some turned east to Falcon Lake, West Hawk Lake, Lake of the Woods, or any of the countless clear rock-bottomed lakes that make up the Whiteshell area. Many families headed north to big murky Lake Winnipeg, with its sandy beaches and rolling waves. We were among those who went north.

While most families went to cabins much smaller than their Winnipeg homes, we went from our crowded little house to a castle at Ponemah Beach. Of course, it wasn't really a castle, and it wasn't really our castle. But, for a few weeks every August, it felt like a castle to us. It belonged to my favourite uncle, my racetrack-owning, cigar-smoking, always-smiling (at least whenever I saw him), fun-to-be-with uncle. My mother had two older brothers, but she was especially close to this one. Back in Winnipeg, he occasionally took the time to stop in to visit my mother during the week. I always liked smelling cigar smoke when I walked in the back door from school because I knew he was there and my mother would be happy. He and my aunt had no children of their own, but they had many nieces and nephews. He liked kids. No one ever really told us that, but we knew it. We could feel it. He always talked to us, asked us what was going on in our lives, and really listened as we told him.

His Ponemah castle was in one of the string of summer communities just south of Winnipeg Beach. It was built on a lakeside lot of about four acres. I think it was originally intended as a camp of some kind, a place that could sleep and feed more than one family at a time. The tree-filled property had lots of room to run and play, even with the variety of buildings scattered around it. Most prominent was the large main house. To us, it was huge with its two big bedrooms, two big bathrooms, an enormous kitchen, an even bigger dining room, a sunroom with a card table, and a sitting room with a massive fireplace. Cozy chairs filled every corner. The card table had an automatic card-shuffler sitting on it. My brother and I liked playing with that card-shuffler so much that we didn't even mind when it rained outside. Years later, after my uncle died, my mother somehow ended up with the card-shuffler and gave it to me. I kept it for a few years, then gave it to my brother. I don't know for sure, but I'd bet money that he still has it.

The main house had a memorable architectural feature: a turret. A ladder consisting of a series of narrow metal rungs ran up the side of the turret. At the top was a platform with a weather vane and probably a terrific view of the lake that I never saw. Every year, when we arrived for our vacation, the first thing my father would say to us was "Remember, nobody climbs up those stairs to the turret." As soon as my father wasn't looking, I knew that my brother would take the first opportunity to take his yearly scramble up that ladder. He tells me now that he never got to the top, but I think he did.

Across a grassy yard from the main house was a series of connected smaller "houses." The first was a shower room that had a little bed in it (I think it might have been for a camp counsellor or a cook or some other service personnel); the next was a freezer house that had an ice-cream cone dispenser on the wall and a freezer full of ice cream in many flavours (including my favourite, Neapolitan); and finally there was a playhouse that stored all the croquet games and badminton sets.

On the lake side of the property was the guesthouse, connected to the main house by a paved path. It had two big bedrooms, each with six single beds, so it had lots of room for us and our cousins and special friends. My siblings and I loved the guesthouse because it was our domain. Our parents stayed in the main house, but we always slept in the guesthouse. Between the bedrooms was a big common room stocked with jigsaw puzzles and a rectangular table to spread them out on. Playing and sleeping in our own separate building was fantastic. We stayed up late jumping on the beds and telling ghost stories. Every once in a while my father would shout from the main house: "Are you kids asleep out there?" We always answered with a loud "Yes, Dad." He would shout back: "That's good. You stay asleep." We could hear him chuckle as he returned to whatever the adults were doing.

At the back of the big common room was the bathroom. What I remember most about that bathroom was the window. Sometimes we crawled through it in the middle of the night to sneak out and clamber over the rocks to the beach. The beach in the moonlight was magical. If we felt particularly brave, we'd dip our toes into the black water, then run out onto the pier and back, but only if the lake was calm. Having seen the roaring surf many times during bad weather, we had a healthy, and necessary, respect for the power of Lake Winnipeg when the wind was up.

The remaining buildings on the property included a double garage and a small tool house where the gardener stored all his equipment. My mother hit the corner of the garage with her car one year. The gardener came to her rescue. He buffed up the bumper of her car and touched up the mark on the garage with some paint. He promised he wouldn't tell my uncle about her little incident, but I'm certain that he did. He was a grizzled man named Nick who was steadfastly loyal to my uncle and made sure that everyone who stayed there treated the place well. He was gruff, but we could tell that he liked us.

Even though our Ponemah castle was located right on the lake and had access to a pier, there was no boat. My uncle had been a bomber pilot in World War II. He had been shot down over the Mediterranean Sea and held as a prisoner of war in North Africa for nine months. He never liked the water after that. We didn't care that there was no boat. We never ran out of things to do at the lake. Ponemah was heaven to us. So much space. So much freedom. The beach. The piers. Our parents relaxed and happy. Packing up to go back to Winnipeg was a sombre task. Summers always came to an end much too soon, and school never failed to start up in September.

Back in Winnipeg, we had a mountain of leaves to rake up every fall. The seven oak trees scattered throughout our yard were very healthy, meaning that we always had at least one full weekend's worth of work to do. My father supervised his young work crew as he built a bonfire in the backyard near the lane. No one used plastic garbage bags back then; no one put leaves out in big bags for the garbage collectors to remove. We burned them. Every weekend in the fall, neighbourhoods all over the city filled with the warm, cozy smell of burning leaves.

Just as we took swimming lessons every summer, we took skating lessons every winter. Starting when I was about six years old, I spent Saturday mornings on the ice at the local outdoor rink less than a block from my house. Unlike today's enclosed neighbourhood arenas, most rinks were outdoors back then. It didn't matter to me; even in Winnipeg's notoriously cold winters, I really liked skating. I liked getting shiny new skates every year. I even liked taking the lessons, because I always wanted to impress my skating teachers, who were usually high school students and therefore, in my eyes, highly sophisticated. I often went skating after dinner during the week just to practise before my next Saturday class.

Aside from the hot chocolate that was always available inside the small community league clubhouse where we warmed our hands by the little metal stove in the middle of the room, my favourite thing about skating was the annual festival. Everyone who was enrolled in skating classes participated in the February show. At least I think it was February, but it could have been January or March. The child somewhere deep in the adult me doesn't know for sure anymore.

What I do know for sure is that every winter all the skating instructors brought their classes together to teach us a routine to perform in the community league festival. One year, the theme of the festival was a winter wonderland fantasy. On second thought, that could have been the theme every year—they all blur together in my head. However, this particular fantasy stands out vividly in my memory not because of the skating skills I mastered, but because of the skating costume I had to wear.

The best skaters always got the starring roles in the festival show. That year, the starring role featured a young girl who wore a pretty outfit with sparkly sequins and a feathery scarf. Our routine had a storyline about a young couple who chased each other playfully through a forest, got lost, got scared, and found each other just in time, just before the big bad woodcutter caught them. What he would have done to them if he had, I don't know and didn't ask.

I wasn't one of the best skaters, so I was assigned to be a tree in the forest. We trees made a grand entrance, moving onto the ice to create the forest by grouping together in various clusters around the rink. During the routine, the playful young couple demonstrated their twirls and figure eights, while we trees showed off our skating skills by shifting a little to the left or the right as the big bad woodcutter spun from one hiding spot to another. Sometimes he bumped into a tree, and she fell over. Some trees fell without the woodcutter's help. Some trees stood out because they were taller than the others. Some merely blended in with the group. I don't remember falling or being knocked down by the woodcutter, and I certainly wasn't tall, so I must have been one of the blenders.

My mother had the most difficult task: she had to make my

costume. I think she might have started out with me as her sewing helper, but my "help" was probably not very helpful. Made entirely of forest green cotton, my tree costume had four parts. The first was a head-to-toe baggy leotard—baggy because it had to go over a winter jacket and leggings. My tree leotard had two arms, two legs, a tight green hood, and snap fasteners down the back. In retrospect, perhaps the leotard should have been made of brown cotton to look more like a tree trunk, but we were head-to-toe green trees.

I thought the branch parts of my costume were the most fun, but I don't think my mother had any fun making them. They consisted of two separate sections, one to go around my waist and the other to go around my neck. Each section had a fabric band that kept the branch snug to my body. Green fabric spanned the space between the band and a wider metal hoop. The neck hoop was a foot or so smaller than the one for my waist. Both branch sections hung down from my body at a slight angle. From the covered metal hoops dangled green cotton fringes. They were meant to look like pine needles, but they looked like green cotton fringes.

Topping it all off was a cardboard cone: think of the Tin Man's hat in the *Wizard of Oz*, but covered in green cotton with another not-quite-needle-like fringe all the way around the brim. I had (and still have) a small head, so the pattern for the hat was a little too big for me. My mother stuffed some crumpled newspaper up into the cone, but the fringe still hung over my eyes. Once out on the ice, I remember that the only things I could see were the skates of the tree in front of me.

After the festival, my mother packed the tree costume away in a box. When I didn't know what I wanted to be the following Halloween, she quickly pulled it out, and I went trick-or-treating as a tree. I remember seeing a few other trees out on our neighbourhood streets that year.

The next year, my mother—the original recycler as far as I'm concerned—didn't miss a beat: my tree getup meant one less Halloween costume she had to come up with. When I protested that I didn't want to wear the same costume two years in a row, she put coloured construction paper ornaments on it, and I trick-or-treated as a Christmas tree. The year after that, I flatly refused to wear the tree costume with or without Christmas decorations, so my middle sister had to be the tree of the year. Being the creative type, she added sparkles to the somewhat tired-looking construction paper ornaments. The year after that, my middle sister refused to wear it, and by this time it was too small for me, so my younger sister had to be the trick-or-treating tree. I don't think my mother ever suggested that my brother be the Halloween Christmas tree, and my youngest sister came along too late to partake in the tree masquerade experience, but three of us remember it well. I don't know what finally happened to that costume. I think one of my sisters might have burned it.

As much as we enjoyed Halloween, the best times in the house with the broken two happened at Christmas. We loved the frenzy of it all. My mother seemed happy, maybe because we were more eager to help with the seasonal chores of baking, shopping, decorating, mailing presents off to Scotland, and delivering parcels to our cousins across the city. I loved to read through the many Christmas cards my parents received, savoured coming home from school to the smells of Christmas goodies and perhaps a big brown parcel of presents that had arrived in the mail.

My parents usually stayed up very late on Christmas Eve wrapping last-minute presents, preparing the stuffing for our turkey dinner, filling our stockings, and assembling the Santa toys for under the tree. On Christmas mornings, my siblings and I would get up very early, sometimes just a few hours after my parents had gone to bed. As the oldest, I was supposed to make sure that we just sat looking at the tree and all the presents, and that we didn't touch anything until my parents got up.

One Christmas, they seemed to stay in bed for a long time, and we just couldn't wait any longer. I went into our parents' bedroom and quietly asked if we could open just one present. I was sure my mother said yes, so I ran back to the living room and we dived in. By the time my parents got up, we had opened every present, even theirs. The toy train they had put together for my brother was broken already, the living room filled from one end to the other with shredded paper, torn ribbons, and crushed boxes. We had no idea who had given us what present. My mother moaned about the generic thank-you notes she would have to write to the aunts: "The gifts you sent the children were very thoughtful." I remember the look on my parents' faces as they stood there staring at the Christmas morning they had missed that year. My siblings and I all felt terrible. It never happened again. After that year, my parents came up with the don't-come-downstairs-before-eight-o'clock rule. No one ever broke it.

✳ ✳ ✳

My sisters and I had a lot of fun the weekend of our high school reunion. Because we all look much alike, people constantly confused us for one another as we mingled in the beer tent, went to sports day in the high school gym, dressed up for the big dinner and dance on Saturday night, had our pictures taken with former classmates, and *oohed* and *aahed* as we recognized familiar old faces.

Yes, the reunion was marvellous, but, for me, the most indelible memory of that weekend remains standing in front of the house that figures so strongly in my family's history. Like a magnet, it drew me inside its walls. I saw not only what it looked like on that day, but also what it had looked like back when it was ours. From the front street, I pictured the daisies poking up along the back lane in the spring, saw the oak leaves piled high around the yard in the fall, smelled the bonfires in the crisp air, felt the first snowflakes of the season fall on my tongue, and heard the sound of my parent's voices calling us in for Sunday dinner. All that reminded me of what it was like to be that family again. And looking at the house number beside the front door, I thought how odd it was that, for the fifteen years we lived there, I had never noticed the broken two.

CHAPTER FIVE

My Mother's Gravy

AT FIRST, MY PARENTS SEEMED largely unfazed by their burgeoning family. In fact, I felt as if they enjoyed having a house full of children. During their few hours of relaxation together on Sunday afternoons, they seldom called out to us by our individual names, instead referring to us as a monolithic group in such comments as "What are you kids up to?" or "You kids better not be getting into any trouble" or "Haven't you kids finished raking those leaves yet?" I even began to think of us as "we kids."

We kids almost always ate our meals at home. The fast-food industry had yet to take hold of North American appetites and families like ours rarely went out for dinner in those days. Questions about shared domestic labour were largely still unasked, so anything inside the house was my mother's job. As a travelling salesman who spent long hours away from home whether on the road or not, my father wasn't around much during the week. On weekends, if the weather was good, he liked to barbecue. Sometimes he made eggs for breakfast on Saturday or Sunday mornings, and he liked to supervise the Sunday night roast beef, but that was the extent of his contribution to household chores.

I don't think my mother ever really liked to cook: she had to. She knew that if she didn't feed her rowdy children well, we would be even harder to manage than we already were. Breakfast and lunch weren't too difficult. At the beginning of the day, it was juice and big bowls of cereal, hot in the winter, cold in the summer. In the middle of the day, cream of mushroom or chicken noodle soup, along with peanut butter or bologna sandwiches, worked no matter what time of the year it was. In all seasons, however, cooking dinner was a testy chore.

Baking was different than cooking. I think my mother enjoyed producing fresh batches of cookies for us to devour after school. I also think she enjoyed making birthday cakes, six each year including one for my father. No one ever had to think about making a cake for my mother because my brother was born on her birthday, so we just added an extra candle to the one she made for him.

We kids insisted on the same birthday cake year after year— a tangy spice cake with a thick, sweet icing we always peeled off and saved for last so that the taste lingered on our tongues. We thought that cake was fancy and exotic. We demanded that cake and only that cake. I think my mother was relieved that no one expected a special new creation each time a birthday loomed on the calendar.

Still, the ordeal of coming up with something for the evening meal was a daily struggle that intensified as our appetites increased. Ever practical, my mother devised a day-by-day menu schedule and followed it to the letter week after week. Sunday's roast beef provided leftovers for Mondays. After that, it was pancakes on Tuesdays, liver on Wednesdays, pork chops on Thursdays, fish sticks on Fridays, hot dogs on Saturdays, which brought us back to Sunday's roast beef again.

In her brief moments of spare time, my mother browsed through magazines she bought during her weekly outing to buy groceries. In the fifties and early sixties, few women's magazines featured articles about female careers. Even the word *homemaking* had yet to make a prominent appearance. Most women in the fifties didn't approach homemaking as a career. I don't think my mother or any of her friends even thought of the word *career* in connection with their lives. They were housewives. After the big flurry of the wedding day and the happy hullabaloo around the births that followed not long afterwards, whether they were called housewives or homemakers didn't really matter as long as they didn't transgress the prescribed expectations for female lives.

Never much of a reader, my mother probably scanned over the sewing hints, glanced briefly at the sweet little fiction pieces, and admired photographs of flower arrangements that might grace some other woman's home. I'm sure she read most of the recipes, maybe skipping over the ones for fancy dishes like soufflés. She couldn't have successfully made a soufflé in our house even if she had wanted to—too many slamming doors.

One year, my mother must have read an article called "365 Ways to Cook Ground Beef." I came to that conclusion because we kids became the experimental mouths on which she tested what seemed like an unending supply of new ground-beef recipes. We didn't particularly like food experiments. As a result, we were a difficult jury, but our unrelenting appetites ensured our participation. Over the next few months, we eliminated all but two of my mother's new recipes, the others not even coming close to anything we would recognize as food.

The first new dish we approved was a meat loaf that had oatmeal in it. It became a staple, thankfully replacing the Wednesday night liver. During the lean years—and there were more than a few—my mother cut back on the meat and beefed up the oatmeal content. My father used to say he didn't know whether to put ketchup or brown sugar on it.

The second recipe we approved was something entirely new to us. Sometime during the fifties, recipes for one-dish casseroles became a new trend. Accompanied by pictures of smiling ladies with perfect hair wearing crisp shirtwaist dresses, women's magazines pointed out the benefits of serving casserole dinners: not only did they result in fewer dishes to wash, but the meal could also be prepared early in the day, allowing plenty of time to do laundry, dust knick-knacks, and polish those pesky floors.

The first time we tried a casserole dinner, my mother silently served us our dinners and disappeared down the hall to await our verdict. Her exit was not unusual. My mother seldom dined with us on weekdays. While we ate at the small grey table in our tiny pink kitchen, she took refuge in the living room, smoking her first cigarette of the day as she settled into the green armchair and her evening ritual of waiting for my father to come home.

Left alone, we kids stared at this weird new food. We always approached experimental meals with our eyes first, taking a very close look at our plates before consenting to taste what was on them. Our standard was simple: it could not look repulsive. If we deemed it visually acceptable, we then placed a token amount into our mouths, but only after making sure the dog was close by in case we needed to dispose of it quickly. We devised a silent signal system so that we could communicate without attracting any attention from my mother down the hall. For the *no* signal, we rolled our eyes as we clutched at our throats with our hands. The *yes* signal was simply to continue eating.

We passed few compliments on to our hard-working cook. She knew our taste test results only by the state of our plates. Empty ones meant she had scored a hit; plates full of picked-at, pushed-around, barely reduced portions meant she had to go back to her magazine pile. One casserole we eventually dubbed "the macaroni thing" soon appeared regularly on our dinner table. This had a downside for my mother. On casserole nights my father started to come home even later. He preferred his meals well done and smothered in gravy.

Over the next few years, we had the macaroni thing a lot. I remember watching my mother make it. Once I even picked up a knife and awkwardly tried to chop a few onions on my own. My mother was patient with my slow efforts for a few minutes, but she soon took the knife out of my hands and sent me off to iron a pillowcase or break up a wrestling match between my brother and sisters.

I don't want to imply that my mother was always at odds with her job to produce meals for her family. I think she liked cooking for special occasions. On birthdays, for instance, although the cake was predetermined, the rest of the menu was usually the birthday child's request. If it was a summer birthday—and this happened often because three of us were born in August—the choice was usually barbecued chicken. Outside meals were always happy ones. My mother prepared the meal's components in the kitchen, and my father prepared the barbecue. We kids revelled in playing around the yard without being hushed or told to "settle down." As dinnertime approached, my mother emerged from the kitchen carrying a tray full of chicken pieces ready for the grill. Then my father took over. Everything my father barbecued—whether garlic toast, baked potatoes, or hamburgers—came off the grill charred black. Blackening was not a gourmet cooking style back then; it's just how my father liked it.

Our barbecue was a typical mid-century primitive. Wobbly black metal legs supported a shallow, round metal dish containing a pile of charcoal briquettes that my father coaxed to a red-hot state using techniques involving starter fluid, matches, and human hot air. A small table beside the barbecue held tongs and two spray bottles: one for water, the other for basting sauce. When the coals were ready, my father placed seven servings of chicken complete with fat-laden skin on the grill and sprayed them with basting sauce. Then he smiled and sank down into his nearby chair to enjoy his drink.

But he wouldn't be there for long because the red-hot coals melted the chicken fat almost immediately. An oily combination of fat and basting sauce flowed down onto the briquettes resulting in a huge flare-up—a flaming orange triangle of stand-back intensity that caused my father to leap out of his lawn chair and squirt our blazing dinner with a blast from the water bottle—all without spilling a drop from his glass. This only temporarily extinguished the flame because the fat continued to drip onto the coals and the whole process started all over again. Sometimes my father grabbed the wrong bottle and sprayed the fire with the basting sauce instead. Those flare-ups were huge: we kids would all scream as my mother ran for the garden hose.

Our dinner always survived somehow, and soon we sat down at the creaky backyard picnic table. Away from the confines of the dining room, my parents relaxed their requirements for reasonable table manners: sometimes we were even allowed to eat with our hands. I always peeled off the charred outer layers to get at the good meat that wasn't burnt. To do this, I had to be first in line, which was not difficult because I was the oldest and still the biggest. After we finished eating, we licked our fingers, ran paper napkins over our greasy faces, and waited for my father to say that the only bad thing about cooking on the barbecue was that there is no gravy. If it was a Sunday dinner, there had to be gravy.

My mother never messed around or experimented with the Sunday dinner menu: roast beef, mashed potatoes, peas, and gravy. My father was always home for dinner on Sundays, and maybe she feared that any variation in the menu might jeopardize his presence. Sometimes Sunday dinner also included popovers or Yorkshire pudding, both of which we consumed eagerly, but even those treats were secondary. The star of Sunday's dinner was always my mother's velvety-smooth gravy. I remember how the dense liquid steamed as it rippled evenly from the spout of the good china gravy boat. The colour alone was food perfected: the same beautiful deep brown of caramel candy or the perfect latte. Unlike restaurant gravies—those thin, pale, washed-out imitations—my mother's gravy was rich, thick, and never lumpy. (I didn't even know that lumps were a gravy issue until I tried to make it myself.) My mother always brought the gravy to the table last because the temperature had to be just right: a little too hot might ruin that amazing texture; a little too cool and, well, cold gravy is just too horrible to contemplate.

At first, we didn't realize how good my mother's gravy was. Perhaps we just didn't think that making gravy was difficult, or perhaps we just didn't think that an ordinary cook like my mother could have a delicate culinary talent. Most likely we just didn't think.

Our family came to appreciate my mother's gravy-making talent one Christmas at my aunt's house. That year, my gentle, soft-spoken aunt cooked the usual festive meal for about twelve people. When the golden-brown turkey appeared on the table, we all crowded to our places, noisily snapped our Christmas crackers, and spread our napkins carefully over our good clothes. As my uncle carved into the big bird, we kids waited eagerly for the finishing touch to arrive. Moments later, my aunt scurried in from the kitchen and placed a little china creamer in the middle of the table. Inside was a pale, runny liquid. I can't remember if we gasped or not, but I do remember the warning look from my father. On the drive home that night, even my mother could not suppress a quiet comment: "I just don't know what happened to her gravy."

After that, we knew that my mother was the ultimate gravy maker. I can still see her at work on her liquid masterpiece: whisk in hand, fist a blur, mining the bottom of the pan for essential morsels of flavour. More than just a sublime version of western civilization's most coveted sauce, the memory of my mother's gravy is also a memory of what we, as a family, too often weren't: united. For a few moments every Sunday evening, my mother had her family's undivided attention as we all waited for the good china gravy boat and its steaming cargo. We kids could hardly sit still as my father carved the roast, placed slices of meat on our plates, and gave the signal that we could help ourselves to what we now knew was the world's best gravy.

I like that Sunday night memory of my mother, try to frame it permanently in my mind's eye. But that picture is often crowded out by another: an indelible image of her profile mirrored on the surface of the chrome teakettle that sat on the stove in the house with the broken two. Always spotlessly polished, its shiny surface provided a wide-angled view of our narrow hallway and the living room beyond. Today, we adult kids can't talk about that kitchen without one of us mentioning the kettle. From our seats at that old grey table surrounded by the pink panelled walls, with the dog sniffing at our feet, whether devouring oatmeal meat loaf or that macaroni thing, we kept our eyes on the kettle's distorted reflection of my mother as she sat smoking in the living room all by herself.

Chapter Six

Beatles and Boyfriends

I HIT PUBERTY IN THE EARLY SIXTIES. Looking back at that time, it seems as if North American society went through a kind of puberty at about the same time as I did. Characterized by rebellion against dominant conservative values and restrictive conformity, the decade of the sixties was exciting, turbulent, and confusing. A youth-fuelled counterculture fed a variety of movements toward widespread social change that ranged from the civil rights movement to anti-war protests to the rise of the women's movement.

Almost everything in the cultural upheavals that define the revolutionary times of the sixties encouraged sexual liberation, but I would soon discover that the rigid social conventions of the 1950s still held firm in our community and family environments. I would also realize that gendered double standards (which still exist today) prevailed despite news-making headlines about sexual freedom: boys were expected to push for sex, and girls were expected to say no; boys were encouraged to experiment and explore their sexuality, but girls were supposed to deny theirs.

I shouldn't really lay the blame for this on the beleaguered mid-twentieth century. It's an age-old situation rooted in many historical injustices. The restrictions placed on women's lives throughout the ages have many manifestations and causes, not the least of which is that women become pregnant. Female sexuality has always been a threat to the organization of any society. The identity of an expected child's mother is usually patently obvious, but men have to rely on women to know for sure who the fathers of their children are. Thus, male-dominant societies have a vested interest in controlling female sexual activity. These things I know now. In the sixties, I had no understanding of sexual politics. I was a mostly cheerful kid expecting that happiness waited for me just around the corner, unaware of the maelstrom I was about to plunge into.

Official agencies in the United States and Canada approved the newly developed birth control pill for distribution in 1960, and much heated debate ensued. Staunch conservatives and an indignant religious community bemoaned the expected loss of morality and traditional values. I remember hearing bits and pieces of the public argument on television and over the radio. I remember seeing articles about it in the newspaper, but I'm not sure if I read them. Numerous questions shaped this contentious public debate, questions that seem absurd today, questions heard repeatedly from the male moderators and talking heads on television: "Why would women want to take birth control pills anyway? Shouldn't nature be allowed to take its course in married sexual relations?" And this particularly noxious comment I found in the CBC archives: "Could any woman be relied on to remember to take a pill every single day?" Somewhere in all this noise, the voices of a few brave souls suggested that the pill should be made available to anyone who wanted it, an argument that merely intensified the already heated debate.

In the sixties, people could not simply walk into a drugstore and buy condoms off the shelf as they can today. Any public display of contraceptives or advertising for birth control information was illegal. For women, access to birth control, or even information about birth control, was available only if they were married, and even then they had to get it from their doctors. Indeed, that is one of the paradoxes of the era: proclamations of sexual liberation abounded during a time when women had no legal access to information about how to protect themselves from unwanted pregnancies, especially if they were unmarried, especially if they were teenagers. The prevailing so-called wisdom of the times deemed that providing birth control information to anyone not married would encourage unwanted sexual experimentation; thus, fear about increased promiscuity was an often-heard argument against mainstream use of what soon became known simply as "the pill." To further complicate things for me, I lived in Winnipeg, a small city deeply connected to its traditional value systems, privy to the goings-on in the rest of the world but not necessarily eager to adopt social change without extended mulling and resistance.

I discovered the details about the sex act where many children of that era did: at school during recess. A friend told me one day while we were sitting in the corner of the schoolyard. She was much more worldly than I. Years later I would think it ironic that she was the only school friend I ever had that my mother didn't like very much.

My mother certainly would not have liked what my friend whispered into my ear that day: "I know where babies come from." I hadn't really thought about where babies came from, but my friend proceeded to enlighten me with a very dramatic description that turned out to be highly accurate. But I didn't believe her. Disturbed, I ran all the way home from school that afternoon. I was eager to ask my mother where her babies came from, certain that she would give me a different answer. My mother had obviously prepared herself for this moment. She handed me a booklet describing the process of menstruation I could expect any day now. Then she told me that when I was married it would be a beautiful thing. Then she smiled at me and said I should set the table for supper.

A few months later, my parents announced at a Sunday night dinner that yet another sibling would be joining our family. I was both excited and appalled. They must have wanted a fifth child very much, I thought, to make themselves do that despicable thing one more time. That may sound falsely naive for a thirteen-year-old by today's standards, but back then, public versions of sexuality were muted, not visible through multiple media forms every second of every day.

I was excited when my mother went into the hospital to have the baby. I looked after the three younger ones as we waited for the news. When my father phoned later that night to say I had a new sister, I thought he would be disappointed that it wasn't a boy because he already had three daughters and only one son. Instead, he sounded like the happiest man in the world.

While my mother was in the hospital, I knew what my primary job was: to cook dinner each night. My mother had stocked the kitchen and left me instructions. The first night I burnt the peas so badly the kitchen filled with smoke. My father laughed when he got home from work. I lamented about how I was going to get the blackened pot clean. Dad solved that problem: he threw it in the garbage and came home the next day with a new one.

The day my mother came home from the hospital, we all waited eagerly to see the baby. When my mother walked in carrying my new sister, we gathered around for our first look at what I thought was the prettiest little face I had ever seen. After a while, my mother put her in my arms: "There you go," she said. "You can practise." And practise I did. We all did. My mother seemed to enjoy watching her older children learn how to take care of a baby under her tutelage. For the next few years, my youngest sister became the focus of life in the house with the broken two. I don't recall any of us being resentful of the attention she got. In my memory, she was a happy little person who drew us all together. Even the dog that became part of our family soon after her birth seemed to like her best. Our little house was definitely more crowded, but I remember our family smiling a lot in those days.

Meanwhile, outside our cozy sphere, there was much going on in the world. I was a very interested spectator. At home, the television had become the focus of our living room. Since getting that first small screen back in 1954, we had definitely become a television-watching family. In 1963, we all watched in sorrow as the United States buried President Kennedy. My mother, eight-and-a-half-months' pregnant with my youngest sister, had been glued to the television for four full days. When I wasn't in school, I was right beside her. We were sitting together on our pink brocade living room sofa when Jack Ruby shot Lee Harvey Oswald right in front of our eyes.

In 1964, The Beatles appeared in our living room three times. They were on the *Ed Sullivan Show*, but to me they were in our living room. Like many North American families, we were Sunday night regulars for Ed's show. My parents never missed it. My father watched all his favourite singers: Louis Armstrong, Nat King Cole, Ray Charles, and Ella Fitzgerald, to name just a few. I had been a little too young in 1956 to fully appreciate Elvis's famous appearance on the show, but I remember watching it. I found "Love Me Tender" a little too mushy and thought "Hound Dog" was a weird song. It would take me a while to become an avid Elvis fan.

In the fifties, my favourite performer on Ed's show had been the little Italian mouse, Topo Gigio. During the early sixties, I remember enjoying performers such as The Jackson Five, The Supremes, and The Temptations. Nothing, however, even came close to equalling those three Sundays in February of 1964, when the fourteen-year-old me lay on the floor very close to the television set so I could see every move The Beatles made. I was a fan: not a screaming idiotic hysterical fan, but a fan nonetheless. My father watched them too, sitting in his usual spot, grousing that this wasn't music. My father had a good musical ear, but he was wrong about those four young Brits.

My friends and I had our own musical heroes closer to home. A band called Chad Allen and the Reflections played around Winnipeg at high school and community league dances. My friends and I followed them around town whenever possible. When "Shakin' All Over" started getting a lot of airplay on the radio, introduced by American disc jockeys as a song from a mysterious band they referred to as "The Guess Who," it wasn't long before Winnipeggers knew that they were hometown to a band with a big future.

Along with the music of the times, I also liked school (but I never would have told my friends). I was a fairly diligent student, but no shining prodigy. I especially liked high school, and especially high school English. For two years, the wonderful David Arnason was my English teacher. I didn't know at the time, and he probably didn't either, that he would go on to become a well-respected Canadian writer. I also didn't know at the time that he is of Icelandic heritage, as am I. Whether or not the Icelandic heritage I shared with my English teacher had a subliminal impact on how I related to high school English, I don't know. What I do know is that, in my favourite class, my favourite teacher made me sit right in front of his desk to lessen my tendency to be distracted by, or cause distractions among, my girlfriends. If I attempted to stray from that location, he would simply point at the vacant seat in front of him until I reluctantly occupied it again. My reluctance was somewhat feigned. I didn't really mind. I liked being closer to his desk, liked his slightly rumpled tweed jackets with their saggy pockets. Pacing back and forth at the front of the classroom, he would jam his hands into his pockets, leaving his thumbs sticking out, twiddling them as he talked. Sometimes he got so involved in what he was saying that he almost seemed to have forgotten his students were there. In those moments, we were totally engrossed in his words.

Even though English was my favourite class, except for Dickens's *Great Expectations* (which I didn't finish reading until much later in my life), I don't remember what other books we studied. But I do remember writing essays. Unlike most of my classmates, I liked writing essays. I kept that to myself too because I didn't want my friends to think I was weird. I remember writing one essay I titled, quite unimaginatively, "Imagination." Something unusual happened to me as I wrote it. Any anxiety I may have felt about the assignment faded into the background. As the words flowed out onto the page, a wonderful new sensation seemed to take control of my hand. The most amazing feeling of satisfaction came over me as I worked on it. I felt like a builder working with exotic material and unusual malleable components as I manipulated words into sentences, sentences into paragraphs, paragraphs into a whole new something, something I made out of nothing but a blank sheet of paper and a pen. I think I had a smile on my face when I handed it in.

The day he returned the marked essays in class, Mr. Arnason (for I can never think of him as anything but Mr. Arnason, even though virtually all his students referred to him as "Arnie") remarked that he had received an essay that was either one of the worst pieces of student writing ever to cross his desk or one of the finest. He said he wasn't sure which of those categories it fell into and paused mid-sentence. Then, with a big gentle smile on his face, he handed me my paper. I can still see the huge red A scrawled across the top of the page.

At the end of class that day, Mr. Arnason asked me to stay for a chat. He asked what I was going to do after high school. He encouraged me to continue writing and suggested that I consider taking an English degree at university. I hadn't thought about it, but I liked the idea. Then he asked if he could keep my essay. I couldn't imagine why he would want it, but said yes feeling pleased that he did. In the decades that have passed since that day, I have often wished that I could read it again and even wondered occasionally what happened to it. Did it go into a trash bin at the end of that school year? Or perhaps into a dusty box where it lies yellowing still? Whatever its fate, although the words have disintegrated completely over time, the feeling they gave me survives.

At home that evening, I told my parents what Mr. Arnason had said about me pursuing English studies at university after high school. They balked. University is very hard and expensive, they said. Even if we could afford to send you to university, why would you study English? they asked. You need some solid training so that you can get a good job in case your husband can't provide for you, they said. We know what's best for our own daughter, they said. They weren't being mean or insensitive, just responding as they thought responsible parents should.

That essay was probably the highlight of my high school career. In school and out, I was an average, unremarkable teenager. I went to movies with my friends, was a cheerleader for the local football team, and babysat the little girl next door for some extra spending money.

One Saturday, a lady who lived down the street from us walked by on her way to work. She was head cashier at the Safeway store on the corner. My father and I were out working in the front yard. Always friendly, Mabel paused to say hello. She asked him how old I was. "Fifteen," he answered. "That's too bad," she said. "We're looking for cashiers, but she has to be sixteen unless you give your approval." "Where do I sign?" said my father.

The next week I started working at Safeway part-time. I made ninety-five cents an hour and thought I was rich. I was a good cashier and liked the customers, many of whom knew my mother or my father or both. The store had a little cafeteria counter right next to the main entrance. I loved sitting there on my coffee breaks chatting with customers and staff. That's where I smoked my first public cigarette, unfortunately for me at the same time as my mother walked through the front door. "What will the neighbours think?" she scolded me later at home.

By this time, I was almost sixteen and had been on a few dates. My parents didn't say much when I started dating. My father smiled a funny little grin the first time a boy came to call for me. My mother told me that she knew I would only go out with nice boys because I was a nice girl. All my life, I had been told to be nice, be helpful, be agreeable, be a good girl and go help your mother. The word *no* wasn't a big part of my vocabulary.

I started going out with my first real boyfriend when I was sixteen. We dated for quite a while, almost two years if I remember correctly. It was that very special first romance. We talked on the phone, visited back and forth at each other's homes, got to know each other's families, went for long walks, and went to school dances together. I was happy.

In 1966, Winnipeg experienced another big flood threat, not nearly as serious as the 1950 flood that was now firmly entrenched in city and family folklore, but one I remember well. The famed Red River Floodway had been under construction for a number of years and was tantalizingly close to being complete. The floodway is prominent in my Winnipeg memories, because arguments for and against it filled the news for several years. Manitoba's then-premier Duff Roblin strongly advocated its construction, but took a lot of criticism from Winnipeggers who felt it was too expensive. Nicknamed "Duff's Ditch," it has now saved Winnipeg from serious flooding time and time again. When it opened in 1969, Duff Roblin was no longer premier so his name isn't even on the official plaque that stands at the start of the floodway. I remember thinking that somehow wasn't right.

After a brutally cold winter, the spring of 1966 was slow to arrive. On March 4, a winter blizzard hit, a huge blizzard, one I can still remember as if it were yesterday because I had the feeling that the snow was never going to stop. The snowdrifts reached as high as my second-storey window. Schools shut down immediately. I was one of the few Safeway employees to make it to work that day. I was also one of the lucky ones to make it home. I lived only a block and half away, but I remember slogging disoriented through the snowdrifts on that walk back to my house. Many Winnipeggers were stranded downtown that Friday night in 1966, sleeping in department stores and restaurants.

When spring arrived a few months later, the river began to rise.

I joined in a sandbagging brigade to protect a friend's low-lying family home. We worked for days and rejoiced when the threat passed and the home was safe. I relished the spirit of community I had felt during those few dike-building days and savoured a sense of satisfaction from being a small part of that effort.

Sometime that summer, my boyfriend suddenly disappeared out of my life with no explanation, no nothing. He just stopped calling me. That September, I discovered that he had even changed schools. Typically self-absorbed as many teenagers are, I made his move to a different school all about me: I thought he was going to great lengths just to avoid me. I was deeply hurt, as devastated as a sixteen-year-old girl can be. In retrospect, I think he was nervous. In the last few weeks of our relationship, we had both started to be curious about sex and perhaps he was unsure about how much longer we could see each other without letting our curiosity take over. Or perhaps he wasn't confident in my ability to say no.

I mended my wounded heart by dating some of the football players I cheered for, but no one really caught my fancy. Then, while I was taking my coffee break at the Safeway lunch counter one day, one of the stock boys sat down beside me. He went to my school so I knew him a little bit, but not very well. He was the quiet type and didn't usually say much. That day he started up a conversation. I told him that one of my girlfriends really liked him and would probably go out with him if he asked. He said that he didn't want to go out with her, but he did want to go out with me. I said no, that my friend would be upset. A few days later, I regretted saying no, but I knew he wouldn't ask me out again. To heck with my friend, I thought. I do want to go out with him, but I knew that this time I would have to ask him instead. He said yes, and soon I had a new boyfriend, one who didn't want me to say no.

Then came 1967: Canada's centennial year. France's President Charles de Gaulle stood on a balcony in Montreal and thundered "Vive Le Quebec Libre," making English Canadians very upset indeed. Despite that uproar, all seemed right with our national world: the Toronto Maple Leafs even won the Stanley Cup that year. The Confederation Train with its special paint job and big maple leaf criss-crossed the country in symbolic unification mode. Bobby Gimbey bounced from sea to sea singing that corny song: "Ca-Nah-Dah, one little two little three Canadians, weeeee love theeeee!" My friends and I decided that it was a dumb song, but we hummed it a lot.

Outside Canada, Elvis Presley married Priscilla Beaulieu in Las Vegas, but he didn't seem to have many musical hits anymore. Other events around the world were very unsettling. The controversy around President Kennedy's assassination continued: Was it a conspiracy? If so, who or what put Oswald up to such a terrible act? Images of the Vietnam War still destroying so many lives on the other side of the world and the protests against that terrible conflict on this side flickered daily across our television screen. Something called a six-day war that happened in the Middle East when the Israeli army clashed with Egypt and Jordan and Syria made everyone nervous. In the United States, race riots broke out in Detroit, then spread to Washington, DC. A fire in an Apollo space capsule killed three astronauts.

Televisions, newspapers, and magazines were full of in-depth coverage about all these events. I knew world news was important, but it hovered only on the periphery of my world. The most important thing in my world was that I would be graduating from high school that year.

CHAPTER SEVEN

Unwed, Not Dead

IN THE SPRING OF 1967, my boyfriend and I went to the prom. The theme was tropical. I can still see the fake palm trees standing in the corners of our high school gym. I can see them because they're in the background of the picture I still have, my boyfriend in his skinny brown suit, me wearing a very unnatural hairdo and a fuschia pink gown that my mother made for me. On the left shoulder of my dress, a yellow corsage is pinned to the shiny, smooth satin. Other than those recorded details, I don't remember much more about prom night: we went, we stayed up late. We weren't into drugs. We probably drank beer, maybe even some lemon gin. I vaguely remember that we borrowed a boat and went for a ride on the Red River in the middle of the night.

And then it was summer. In sixties mythology, the summer of 1967 is often referred to as the summer of love. Against a backdrop of violence across the globe, hippie counterculture flourished. Bead-wearing, flower-bearing, long-haired young people flocked to San Francisco, New York, Toronto, Montreal, Vancouver, any major North American city proclaiming revolution, alternative living, communal love, creative expression, and sexual freedom.

In Winnipeg, many people were caught up in the excitement of hosting the Pan-American Games. I hardly noticed the games were happening, although I think I did go to one swimming event. I worked my shifts at Safeway, went out with my boyfriend, hung out with my friends, and played my little transistor radio non-stop. "Shakin' All Over" still played regularly on local radio stations. I know all the words by heart even today: "When you move in right close to me . . ." My music that summer was all about love: "All You Need Is Love" sang my favourite band (still The Beatles); "To Love Somebody" sang the Bee Gees; "Light My Fire" sang Jim Morrison and the Doors; "Let's Spend the Night Together" sang the Rolling Stones.

For my friends and me, love definitely was the theme of our summer. The adult community around us left us pretty much alone. As long as we showed up for our part-time jobs and didn't cause any trouble, we could do anything we wanted. So we did. My boyfriend had moved out of his parents' house into a basement apartment he shared with a friend. My memory is somewhat fuzzy here, but I think that's where we finally had sex, on a little bed in that apartment. Afterwards, I do remember being puzzled about what all the fuss was about. I wasn't even certain we really had "gone all the way." If we had, I thought (and kept this thought to myself), this thing called sex was a little disappointing. I know we did it several more times, but I don't really remember how many. I know that I liked lying beside him afterwards, but I don't recall what we said to each other. What I do remember, vividly, is that by the time summer was over, by the time the leaves started to change colour, by the time I walked across the stage at my high school gymnasium to receive my diploma that fall, I knew I had a problem. I was, to use a common euphemism of the times, a girl "in trouble."

I didn't tell anyone for a while. Then I told my boyfriend. We walked around for a few weeks hoping it wasn't true. When I finally confessed to my mother, she accepted my news with dismay. After a few days of thundering silence, my parents called me into the living room to talk about it. What were they to do? I couldn't stay at home during my pregnancy. They had my brother and sisters to consider. Besides, what would the neighbours think? I already knew that asking to have my baby come into our family was out of the question. By this time, it was obvious to me that my parents were struggling a little, almost overwhelmed with five children and limited financial resources. My sense was that they were waiting for some of their kids (starting with me) to move out of the house, not to have more move in.

One thing my parents were very clear about was that they definitely didn't want me to get married. They hadn't been too sure how much they liked my new boyfriend before this; they certainly liked him a lot less now. More than that, however, a sudden marriage would have meant public shame. The neighbours wouldn't have to speculate about anything; they would know. A wedding would also have meant that my parents would have to tell my grandparents about my condition, and I don't think either one of them could face that: the furrowed brows, the rigid disapproval, the silent reprimands for failing as parents.

In the midst of all this uncertainty, I did my best not to think about my situation. Mostly I tried not to think about my baby. My youngest sister was only four years old. From the time I had spent looking after her, I knew that I could care for and love a baby, but I was afraid to figure out how to love the one growing inside me. During this time, my parents said little to me. After our conference in the living room, an uneasy silence settled around the household. My mother sighed a lot. My father wasn't home very much. Soon I realized that I was going to have to come up with a solution myself.

Unmarried women did not keep their babies in the sixties. I was to discover during the next year that any young woman in my situation who dared to say that she might keep her baby was immediately discouraged from doing so. Whether from a parent, a doctor, or a social worker, the message was always the same: you have nothing to offer a child; you're not ready to be a mother; you're being selfish; you'll be ruining his or her chances for a good life; you'll have more children when you're ready and forget all about this one.

Underlying these professional words of advice was also the tacit suggestion that an unmarried teenaged girl who was pregnant either lacked good moral character or was psychologically deficient, or both. So, in the absence of encouragement from our families and our communities to keep our babies, those of us who found ourselves pregnant and unwed had three choices. One was to get married. Another was to find someone to perform an illegal abortion. The third choice was to have the baby and surrender it to an adoptive family, a properly married couple whose marriage licence gave them instant credibility as parents.

At the end of that summer, I had started a job with a bank in downtown Winnipeg. As I was young and healthy, my pregnancy didn't show for several months. When my stomach began to protrude a little, fashion was on my side. The dress styles at the time were loose and fortunately for me, the tent dress was in. My mother had mentored me into a pretty good seamstress, so I made myself a couple of big billowy dresses to wear to my clerking job on Portage Avenue, not far from the famous intersection with Main Street.

Travelling back and forth to work on the bus each day, I would think about my dilemma. While I was somewhat curious about what it would be like to be a married woman, I don't think I particularly wanted to get married at age eighteen. When I thought about marriage, I saw my parents' difficult relationship, saw how my father's frequent absences too often left my mother angry and resentful. I thought about standing in the kitchen drying dishes as my mother washed them (no dishwashers in those days), all the while muttering to herself through clenched teeth: "If it wasn't for you kids . . ." I thought about my father coming home many nights looking tired only to be greeted by a horde of clamouring, sometimes cranky kids and their fuming mother. Marriage, as far as I could see, didn't look like much fun for either the husband or the wife.

I didn't think long on the abortion option. Although it would be removed from the Criminal Code in 1969, abortion was still illegal in Canada in 1968. My friends and I had all heard horror stories about botched abortions and self-inflicted abortive techniques. When I imagined searching for a doctor to perform an abortion, I saw a dark alley, a sly exchange of cash, a dirty back room, and an unshaven, smelly man wielding menacing tools. As little as I knew about myself at that time, I knew one thing for sure: I was a coward. I didn't want to get an abortion—didn't even like to think about it.

My aversion to abortion was more than just being terrified about the process itself. I also knew that I didn't want to harm the little life growing inside me. I wanted to do everything I could to make sure that my baby was born healthy. I didn't realize at the time that I was already feeling what my society was convinced I couldn't offer my child: maternal love.

Uncomfortable at home, I walked a lot in those days, sometimes by myself, sometimes with a girlfriend, often with my boyfriend. He didn't like coming around our house much anymore. I didn't know until years later that, when he came to see me one day, my mother answered the doorbell, slapped him across the face, and slammed the door shut. So he and I would meet somewhere and roam the streets of our neighbourhood, talking about the lives we saw spanning out in front of us, about what we wanted out of them, and sometimes about what we should do about our dilemma.

I remember that we talked around the pregnancy a lot, instead of directly about it. But one night, we did speculate about just taking off and getting married despite my parent's opposition. At the end of that walk, I thought we had decided that was what we were going to do; however, neither of us ever brought up the subject of marriage again. I suppose if I had insisted that he marry me, he would have, but I wasn't about to trap anyone. I suppose if he had insisted I marry him, I would have, but he was probably as confused as I was about marriage and what he could offer a child.

Apparently, there was another option I didn't know about at

the time. I didn't find out until much later that, sometime during the first few months of my pregnancy, my boyfriend's parents came to our house to meet with my parents. When they offered to take my baby and raise it themselves, my parents stood up and asked them to leave. I don't know why my parents reacted that way, but I doubt that it was because my boyfriend's parents wanted my baby without me, its mother, which I think would have been my contribution to the conversation had I been asked to be part of it. I will never know what went through my parents' minds that night. My father is gone now and, except for one tension-filled conversation years later, my mother has steadfastly refused to talk about that time in our lives.

So I was left with one choice: adoption. In the fifties and the sixties, adoptions were predominantly managed through the closed adoption system, a process premised largely on silence and secrecy. Before World War II, maternity homes and social workers involved in adoption at least made small attempts to work toward keeping single mothers and their babies together by offering young women shelter before and after their babies were born, offering them a place to bond with their babies, offering them time to consider the consequences of their decision.

As cultural paradigms congealed into the rigid model of the ideal middle-class family after the end of World War II, the attitudes of social agencies and maternity homes changed. Girls like me were not young women who needed a helping hand. Instead, we were seen as somehow delinquent and definitely unfit as mothers. The focus of social agencies became one of securing babies for those ideal middle-class couples who were struggling to conform to the modern model of family, but couldn't because of infertility problems. In some areas of North America, this demand for newborn babies resulted in an ominous moniker for the times: the Baby Scoop Era. For married couples seeking children they couldn't have, the closed adoption system provided babies along with a guarantee that the biological parents would never be heard from again. For the families of unwed mothers, the closed adoption system provided a way to avoid social stigma. On the surface, the system seemed to offer them a rational solution, a way out of a difficult situation. No one noticed how rooted it was in rigid, even irrational, notions about what families should look like.

I didn't think about these social and cultural contexts at the time. Caught in an untenable situation, in a bed of my own making as my mother reminded me the few times she actually spoke to me about it, I didn't know I could insist on different options, that I could insist on my rights as a mother-to-be, that I should expect support instead of silent condemnation from both my family and my community at large. Those things never crossed my mind. So, on a crisp winter day, having quietly resigned my job at the bank, my tent dresses no longer hiding my condition, I slipped into one of those mid-century relics, a maternity home.

To call these places maternity homes is a highly ironic misnomer: maternity homes were not homes, nor did they function to promote maternity. They were institutions to house and hide those deemed maternally inappropriate. Also known as homes for unwed mothers, they were busy places in those days; Winnipeg, a small city, had three of them. I didn't know their exact locations, but I knew they were out there somewhere. Although hidden, teenage pregnancies were a bit of an epidemic at the time, so much unofficial information about these mysterious, foreboding places floated around my circle of friends.

Fortunately for me, the one I served my time in was not dingy and dank, but clinically clean and tolerable with a cool, no-nonsense atmosphere. Driving up to its door the first time, I was relieved to see a nice little building. I had been expecting a brooding old place, something creepy, dark, and gothic. Instead, I found myself in a fairly new building, low and sleek in mid-century modern style. Located on a secondary highway on the outskirts of Winnipeg, safely on the opposite side of the city from my neighbourhood, its site was secluded, the building set well back from the main road on a small plot of land surrounded by trees.

Sparsely furnished throughout, the main wing had a common room with a number of sitting areas, a dining area with several big round tables, and a spacious kitchen where we all pitched in to prepare the meals. The bedroom wing had two single beds in each room with a big common washroom at the end of the hall. A roster sheet was posted on a bulletin board assigning domestic chores to each girl, more rigorous ones like vacuuming and cleaning bathrooms to the newer arrivals, lighter ones like dusting to those further along in their pregnancies.

Although I certainly felt lonely, once I settled in I also felt relief. I was able to relax there somewhat, to recover from the stress of hiding my growing belly, of avoiding friends and family. During the four months I spent at the maternity home, my outings were few. My boyfriend worked a lot of hours because he was paying for my room and board. But he came to visit me about once a week, borrowing his best friend's car to take me out for a drive after dark. Occasionally we went to a drive-in movie.

One day I received a parcel in the mail. It was from my boyfriend's mother. She sent me a pretty little nightgown and a few other small items. Included was a short note hoping that I was doing well. I was pleased with this unexpected gift. I hope I sent her a thank-you note. I'm not very good at thank-you notes.

During those months, I rarely saw my parents. I remember they drove out one Sunday afternoon to see me, but they wouldn't come inside the building even though it had a large comfortable visiting area. They sat in the car while I stood wrapped in a big borrowed coat and talked to them through the window. One of my sisters thinks that she and all my other siblings were in the back seat, but she's not certain and I don't remember. It's entirely possible because Sunday afternoon drives were a common family activity.

I don't mean to make my parents sound cold and unfeeling. I know that they felt my situation deeply; however, they largely dealt with my pregnancy through deft avoidance. They told any family and friends who noticed my absence that I was away on a trip and just hoped no one asked too many questions.

For the most part, the maternity home staff (to us, they were "den mothers") were distantly pleasant to its occupants, or inmates as we jokingly referred to ourselves. One warm exception was a part-time den mother who lived nearby and often invited the girls to come to her house for coffee and games. Sympathetic to our plight, she was at ease with us, non-judgmental in both her words and her actions. We liked the nights when she was on duty.

Although the home discouraged too much familiarity among its residents, most of us became instant friends anyway. I remember that we laughed a lot. The prevailing public image of an unwed mother was of a bad girl who should hang her head low, acknowledge her shame, and adopt an attitude of atonement for her supposed lapse in character, but I never felt that image had anything to do with me at all, and I don't think the other girls did either. As far as we were concerned, in a rigid social order filled with inequities, double standards, and conflicting messages, we were just the ones who got caught.

As we served our time banished from our communities, we created moments of fun in our situations, playing pranks on one another, forming strong alliances. We took long walks down the rural highway nearby, telling ourselves as we went that we were exiles, not prisoners. To while away the evenings, we sat together in the front room. As we chatted, we kept our hands busy by knitting, making crazy long scarves for our friends instead of booties and bonnets for our babies. I remember some of us sitting in that room one evening when the den mother on duty scolded a girl she had caught in a passionate embrace with her boyfriend at the front door. The girl responded with a fiery "I'm unwed, not dead," and stomped off down the hall. We all turned away to hide our grins and that phrase became our shared mantra.

We shared our stories and our fears with each other. Most of us knew very little about what was going to happen to us during labour and delivery. The home provided some instruction about the birthing process, but that information was limited to pictures in medical books. The staff told us to direct our questions to the doctor who made weekly visits to the home to see us so that we didn't have to go out and see him. Nevertheless, although he was a kind man who said we could ask him anything, most of us were either too uncomfortable to give voice to any questions we did have or didn't know what questions we should be asking. As a result, anything we learned about what was going to happen to our bodies usually came from each other.

Despite my relative comfort, the months dragged by. I can't remember what the day-to-day weather conditions were, but it felt like winter was reluctant to give in to spring that year. My due date came and went. No baby. One week passed. I paced up and down the hall day and night. Another week passed. Still no baby. I began to think pregnancy was to become my permanent condition.

When I finally went into labour late one night early in May, only one den mother was on duty at the home, so she sent me to the hospital in a taxi by myself. Once admitted to the maternity ward, I spent my time in the labour room alone. At first, the contractions were quite mild and I was fairly calm. Nurses came in to check on me, busy and officious. Eventually the pains became more intense, closer together, and then pounded right on top of each other. Suddenly a host of nurses appeared in my room, focused intently on my body but somehow not on me.

When they wheeled me to the delivery room, I grew frightened and began to cry. Very quickly, my crying turned into screams of panic. The nurses tried to calm me down. Then the doctor arrived, a man I had never seen before. He didn't speak to me, but I remember that he asked the nurses what all the fuss was about. One nurse replied that I was "one of those unwed mothers from the home." "Well," he said, "just put her out and let's get on with it." (As strange as it seems now, back in the sixties, most North American women gave birth while under a general anaesthetic.)

When I woke up, all was calm and I was on a stretcher. The doctor was nowhere in sight, but several nurses still bustled around me. What happened? I asked. You had a little boy, they said. Is he all right? I asked. Yes, he's fine, they said. Can I see him? I asked. No, that's not wise, they said.

The next day, I wandered the halls until I found the nursery section. I looked in all the nursery windows until I saw my name written on the end of a bassinet, a beautiful baby boy sleeping peacefully inside it.

I wasn't supposed to hold my baby, much less feed him. Every day, when the nurses brought hungry babies to the three other mothers in my room, I left and went down the hall to stand at the nursery window. For the next five days (as strange as it seems now, back in the sixties, North American women usually stayed in the hospital for four to six days after giving birth), this was my routine.

The day before I left the hospital, a nurse came to me and said that I had to give my son a name. I had known this would happen. I had heard about the hospital's naming ritual during my stay at the home. I knew that I would be told that the hospital needed a name for their paperwork. But every time I thought about naming my baby, my mind shut down. Finally faced with the moment, I stalled for a few minutes. I asked the nurse why I had to name him when he wasn't going to be mine. She gave me a stern look that I can still see. I don't know whether she actually said these words, but this is what my memory hears anyway: "You don't even want to give him a name?"

What I didn't tell the nurse is that I did want to name my son. Even though I knew the family who adopted him would change it, I wanted to give him a good name, a name from me that bode well for him. But, unlike "normal" mothers, I couldn't spend time during my pregnancy thinking about names. When I thought of my child, I didn't want to think of a he or a she, but I also didn't want to think of it as just "it." So, while I was pregnant, I called my baby "Bump." When I patted my belly, I patted "Bump." Sometimes when I lay awake in bed late at night, I talked quietly to "Bump"; sometimes "Bump" would respond with a kick.

But the nurse standing in front of me with the form I had to fill out dangling from her hand was not going to accept "Bump" as a name, and I had only a few minutes to come up with something good enough for a baby I would never see again, who would probably never know what names I chose for him. Looking down at the wristbands around my arm, I noticed the delivery room doctor's last name. I asked the nurse if she knew what that doctor's first name was. She did. So I named my baby after the two doctors who had tended to me: the kindly doctor who came to visit me in the maternity home and the doctor who delivered my baby. As the nurse walked away with the completed paperwork, I said my baby's new name out loud to myself. I liked the way it sounded, dignified but friendly, the name a little boy who might grow up to be a doctor would have.

If I had kept him, I would have given him a different name. Had we been raising our son, my boyfriend and I likely would have had fun deciding what to name him. I would have made an argument for the boy name I liked the best at that time of my life: Steven. My boyfriend would have thrown his favourite boy name into the mix, but I have no idea what that might have been because we never talked about naming our child. I think we would have come up with something that honoured both our son's individuality and our families. I had a healthy list of names to choose from, names from my family's multiple histories, names that held a host of stories about the family that he should have been part of.

The day I was released from the hospital, I returned to the maternity home. Over the next twenty-four hours, I gave away all my tent-shaped clothes, packed my little white suitcase, and said goodbye to friends I would never see again. Once our babies were born, maternity home friendships usually dissipated for good. As unobtrusively as I had slipped inside its walls, I slipped out and returned to my family.

Almost without comment, I soon fell back into the familiar daily routine of our household. I think my sisters and brother were happy to see me, but it was clear to me that they had been told to ask me no questions about my absence. In turn, I offered them no explanations. I complied with the instruction I had received from my mother back in the hospital, that my father expected silence from me on the topic of my pregnancy. Several decades would pass before I ever dared to talk to my sisters about this episode in my life.

Back in the sixties, the birth of a child had yet to become the highly documented family event it is today, eagerly attended by fathers, birthing coaches, grandparents, digital cameras, and video recorders. Back then, happy parents usually waited until the day mother and baby were released from the hospital to record images of the new arrival. Nevertheless, most hospitals did have professional photographers on staff so that proud new moms could order their babies' first official portraits. While I was still in the hospital, a photographer visited all the mothers offering to take baby pictures. The day he came to our ward, he somehow knew not to stop at my bed. In what was for me a surprisingly assertive moment, I followed him down the hall and convinced him to take a picture of my baby. I gave him all the money I had— I think it was about $1.25—and my home address.

I knew that my parents would not have wanted me to have such a painful reminder of this period in my life, so I remained on watch for the postman after I returned home. Fortunately, the day it arrived, I was at home babysitting my little sister and got to the mail before anyone else. That picture was, and still is, a stunningly beautiful photo of my infant son, his eyes wide open. After staring at him for a very long time, I put the picture and the two identification bracelets I had worn in the hospital—one for me, one for him—in the envelope the picture came in and placed that package in my night table drawer. As I write this, it's still there, in a different night table, but the same small envelope, somewhat yellowed by now, my old Winnipeg address handwritten in a casual scrawl across the centre, a cancelled pink stamp that cost four cents in the top right-hand corner.

As for my extended family, once I returned, none of my aunts or uncles or anyone else inquired about my "trip"; in fact, not many people inquired about my absence at all, so explaining it was not difficult. It was as if my first pregnancy had not happened; I could simply pretend it away. The silent approach to my situation fulfilled my parents' one condition for my return to the family fold: Do not talk about it. Except for the small black-and-white picture of a wide-eyed infant tucked deep into my night table drawer, the stretch marks on my breasts, and a strange emptiness that hovered uneasily in and around my thoughts, I could wrap up the entire experience, stow it somewhere deep in my psyche, and hope that time would dull my memory.

The world outside Winnipeg hadn't calmed down in my absence. In Canada, one month before my baby's birth, Canada's justice minister, Pierre Trudeau, approved amendments to the Criminal Code that legalized, among other things, abortion and contraception. The state, he famously said, had no business in the bedrooms of the nation. A few years earlier, I wouldn't have known what he meant. Now I did.

In the United States, one month before my baby was born, Martin Luther King had been assassinated in that fabled music city of Memphis, Tennessee. One month after my baby was born, Robert Kennedy was assassinated in Los Angeles. Two days later, James Earl Ray was arrested in London for the murder of Dr. King. A few weeks later, newly promoted to prime minister of Canada, Mr. Trudeau called an election, launching the summer of Trudeaumania.

Although I followed these events, I felt somewhat detached from everything going on in the world around me.

My parents sent me on a short trip to Montreal to visit my grandparents. Shielded from knowledge of my pregnancy, they hovered over me as if I were a delicate treasure. We went on a drive to see the sights of Old Montreal. They sat in the back of their chauffeured car while I walked up the steps of St. Joseph's Oratory. They took me to their favourite Montreal restaurants and proudly introduced me to a few of their friends. They lamented the fact that they didn't know anyone my age they could invite to dinner. One night, they asked me how I liked my job at the bank. They were mildly perplexed when I told them I had quit, but they didn't ask for details and said they were certain I would find something soon.

Back in Winnipeg, on a hot July day, I was tanning in our backyard when the beautiful St. Boniface Cathedral caught fire while under renovation. I didn't see the fire itself, but the smoke smell hung over the city for days. On my radio, The Guess Who had a Canadian hit with "These Eyes," a beautiful ballad, a song that I would normally take to immediately, but I was strangely untouched by its emotion. In fact, I noticed that I was unusually calm inside, too calm. I missed feeling my baby inside me, moving around my tummy, but other than that I didn't feel much of anything at all. It was as if some part of me had been amputated or gone numb. It'll pass, I thought. I remembered what the den mothers at the home and the social worker had told me: it'll be like it never happened, you'll have other children, you'll forget about this one. I didn't yet recognize the biggest lie I've ever heard. Birthmothers never forget.

A year went by. On the radio, it was the Age of Aquarius urging everyone to "Let the Sunshine In." Sometime shortly after his first birthday, I must have signed the final adoption papers. For years afterwards, I wouldn't be able to remember that moment at all. On the subject of my baby and the adoption, I had held to my promise of silence. In fact, I held to it so well that I had even silenced myself.

I was completely immersed back into my life by this time, but nothing was ever the same again. I saw and heard the world around me differently than I had before. When I was at home, I stayed in my room a lot. On my radio, Aretha Franklin taunted me with "Chain of Fools." If I didn't like what was on the radio, I had a small portable record player in my closet and a modest collection of albums. Over and over again, I played Simon and Garfunkel's *Sounds of Silence*: "I am a rock," I sang along with Paul and Art. "I am an island . . ." In September that year, the radio airwaves were full of a new single by Diana Ross and the Supremes: "Love Child." I could hardly stand to listen to it.

To me, it seemed as if 1967's summer of love had been replaced by a less naive, more sombre tone. Everything felt so turbulent. Or maybe it was just me. I didn't know, so I put my head down and did what my social environment conditioned me to do: buried my feelings and carried on with my life.

CHAPTER EIGHT

Three Years

ALTHOUGH SIMONE DE BEAUVOIR'S *The Second Sex* made its appearance in France the same year I was born, I would remain unfamiliar with it for more than forty years. When Betty Friedan's revealing book about the North American housewife, *The Feminine Mystique*, was published in 1963, I was busy becoming a Beatles fan and babysitting my four younger siblings. It's too bad I didn't read Friedan's work back in the sixties because I think even the uninformed teenaged me would have recognized my mother's life, especially in the chapter about "the problem that has no name." I might have understood my mother sooner, had more sympathy for her constant weariness and sudden moods. I might even have been able to help her deal with the resentment that sometimes seemed almost ready to consume her.

But neither my mother nor I read any of the big feminist texts that launched the women's liberation movement in the sixties when they were first published. And I didn't read Adrienne Rich's courageous work about motherhood and mothering, *Of Woman Born*, until the 1990s, although it was published in 1976. In 1976, I was a mother myself, my time occupied at home with three very young children. Any reading I might have been doing then would have been related to childcare, vegetarian cooking, or *The Cat in the Hat*. Any writing I did was probably in the form of a grocery list.

As my life progressed, I occasionally thought that feminism had passed me by. I wondered why, although I knew it was happening, feminism somehow didn't seem relevant to me. Back in 1966, when I was preoccupied with schoolwork, my part-time Safeway job, and learning new routines for the cheerleading squad, I was unaware that, in New York, charter organizers of the fledgling National Organization for Women (NOW) had gathered in a small borrowed room filled with second-hand furniture and blue-jean-clad women. Nor did I know that in Canada, women's groups had formed across the country, beginning with the 1967 establishment of the Toronto Women's Liberation Movement, and followed soon by Simon Fraser University's The Feminine Action League, and Vancouver's Women's Caucus. At the time, I thought the women's movement was all about the birth control pill. Like many of my friends, my simplistic teenaged assessment of the first ripples of second-wave feminism was that women finally had sexual freedom. We didn't know yet how confining that freedom could be.

Simply put, I was sadly uninformed about the groundbreaking efforts of so many women during those times. I was completely unaware that, in academic circles on both sides of the Atlantic Ocean, critical approaches to literary theory had exploded in response to many stimuli, perhaps primarily the American civil rights movement of the early 1960s. A burgeoning amount of intellectual work produced by female thinkers, many of whom had fought for and found admittance into the male-dominated realm of English literature academia, led to the development of a new discipline in theoretical analysis: feminist literary criticism. This new discipline disrupted long-held notions that the assumed reader, writer, and critic of literature was male, a thought that had never crossed my teenaged mind even though I read a lot. While new ideas stirred everywhere else in the world, I was snug in my little life, completely absorbed in myself.

I'm not saying that I lived in a vacuum. I didn't. I swam in the ideological waters of my community, but didn't even realize I was swimming, much less what the water was like. News reports occasionally featured examples of early second-wave feminism as it began its rise to the front pages of the 1970s. Although I did read the newspapers that came to our house every day, I must have focused my attention on the comics section or the movie reviews. In retrospect I see that, at the end of what I naively thought was a sophisticated high school experience, I was largely distanced from, and uninformed about, feminism and the potential it had to affect my life. I say now with certainty that, had there been a Canadian equivalent of a groundbreaking feminist book published during those years, I might have heard about it, but I doubt that I would have read it. Looking back, I think it's too bad that I didn't read those *Chatelaine* magazines lying around the house more carefully, because then-publisher Doris Anderson was putting out some very progressive feminist writing between the covers of that conventional domestic package.

Back in the summer of 1968, after my pregnancy and the adoption, I had to decide what to do next. I didn't want to go back to working at the bank. I didn't want to go back to being a cashier at Safeway. I had my high school diploma showing some very reasonable marks, so I knew I could get into university. I wanted more education, but I was also aware that my parents were struggling financially. Although they kept up a brave front, I knew that my mother felt that they had become the "poor" branch of their extended families. This was hard for them. My parents had both come from well-to-do homes. All their siblings seemed to have built successful lives for themselves. My parents had produced the most children, but financial stability eluded them. The warm glow that had surrounded our family for a few years after my youngest sister was born had dimmed somewhat. I felt more than a little responsible for that.

After I had been back home for a month or so, my mother told me that my uncle had offered to pay my tuition so I could go to university. She said I could accept his offer if I wanted to, that it was my decision, but she warned me that going to university was very expensive, that university work was very hard, and that it would mean going to school for four more years. I was torn. I did want go to university, but I didn't want to make my father feel badly for needing my uncle to pay my way. As well, after what I had put my family through, I certainly didn't feel as if I was worth my uncle's investment.

I finally decided to apply to vocational school to become an x-ray technician instead. It was cheaper than university and only two years of study instead of four. I was accepted immediately and started classes at Winnipeg's Red River Community College that September. I threw myself into my classes and worked hard. I wanted to do well.

My distractions were few. My boyfriend had left Winnipeg to follow his family out west, so we didn't see much of each other anymore, but we did keep in touch. I went to visit him for a weekend once. We had a good time together, but after that visit, our relationship began to dwindle. It wasn't that I no longer cared for him. I did. It was that I couldn't look at him without thinking of our child. With several provinces between us, we soon drifted apart. In fact, even back in Manitoba, I drifted away from most of my high school crowd at this time. A few of my close friends knew about my pregnancy, but had sworn never to tell anyone. Still, I didn't know whether rumours had leaked out about it. If they had, I didn't want to know.

That year, my musical hometown heroes, The Guess Who, released their beautiful tune "Undun." It plunged into my head so deeply that I began to think that Randy Bachman had written it for me: "She didn't know what she was headed for . . . She's gone too far. She's lost the sun. She's come undun . . ." I was determined that I wouldn't be a girl who spent the rest of her life "undun." I wanted to put some distance between my high school years and me. In fact, I was yearning to put some distance between my family and me, between Winnipeg and me.

Working as a student technician in the x-ray department of a Winnipeg hospital, I became friendly with a couple of cheery co-workers. One of my new friends introduced me to a group of student pilots training at the base in Gimli, a small Lake Winnipeg town about an hour north of the city. One of them asked me to go out with him. The next weekend, another one asked me out. Soon I was dating regularly again. I liked these guys a lot, but not romantically. I didn't want to have sex with them. I didn't want to have sex with anyone. I liked them because they were confident and sure of themselves. I liked them because they lived, at least from my perspective, exciting lives. I liked them because they knew nothing about my past. I had fun going out with them, perhaps partially because, at this point in my life, I was better at dating. I had figured out how to say no.

One weekend, I was part of a group that went to a party at the Officers Mess on the base in Gimli. From our table across the room, I spied someone new. I watched as he entertained everyone at the bar with jokes. He didn't seem to be with a girl so I asked who he was. Everyone at my table knew him. He was one of the flying instructors and a great guy, they all agreed. That one, I thought. That's the one I want.

Later on that week, I was thrilled when he asked me to go out with him. He was tanned, handsome, and different from anyone I had ever known. And he was funny. I laughed easily when I was with him. Soon I couldn't wait for each weekend to come so I could see him. We went to see the newly released movie *M*A*S*H* and laughed together until we couldn't talk, sitting in the theatre long after the credits had finished rolling. When we started to get a little more serious, I told him about my pregnancy; he was unperturbed and did not judge me. I was hooked. I invited him home for Sunday dinner. He brought flowers and special bottle of sherry for my mother. My parents were instantly impressed. My brother and sisters warmed up to him and laughed at all his jokes. He went with me to walk my little sister across the football field for her swimming lessons. Spring and early summer were good for me that year. But, as suddenly as he had come into my life, he was gone. The Canadian Armed Forces doesn't let romance interfere with their operations; they transferred him to a base in Ontario. He left almost immediately.

Meanwhile, my parents had decided to move the family to Calgary. My father had been offered a job there, and I think they were excited about the opportunity for a fresh start. Also, my grandparents had moved to Calgary from Montreal the year before, back to the city they had lived in when their children were born. They were getting older, and my father wanted to be closer to them. My brother and two of my sisters were not happy about the move. They were high school age and did not want to leave their friends. My little sister didn't care about moving. It was an adventure for her. I didn't care about moving away from Winnipeg either. I was planning to leave anyway. I remember taking a picture of our house with a "For Sale" sign in front of it. I can't find that picture anymore, except in my memory.

And so it was that, at the end of summer 1970, with a smiling six-year-old between them in the front seat, three sullen teenagers and a dog in the rear, my parents took their overloaded car, with the family snowmobile on a trailer behind it, out to the Trans-Canada Highway and turned west. With my x-ray training complete, I boarded a plane to go on a trip, a real trip this time. I flew to Scotland to attend my cousin's wedding and stayed for seven months, living with my aunt and uncle, working for several of those months at the Western Infirmary in Glasgow.

Life with my Scottish family was completely different from life with my family in Canada and yet somehow oddly familiar:

familiar because they treated me as one of their own, familiar because I recognized my grandparents and my father in the framed pictures around the house, and unfamiliar because their house was nothing like ours. They lived in what felt like a marvellous mansion, a big, two-storey stone dwelling filled with comfortable furniture and fireplaces, so roomy that it made the house with the broken two look like a garden shed. Scattered throughout the house were numerous clocks of various sizes. They all chimed on the hour and some of them every fifteen minutes as well. My uncle was a clock aficionado. He especially liked their chiming sounds, so he deliberately set all the clocks to different times. At any given moment, in some room somewhere in the house, a clock announced the time. Time was important there because every resident of that house had a different schedule. Comings and goings never stopped. All my cousins had their own little cars. The driveway was seldom empty, with compact right-hand-drive vehicles zooming in and out regularly.

I adored my gregarious aunt and my hearty Scottish uncle. I called him Big Daddy. He was a gentle, kind man, smiling and patient with everyone in his family, especially his wife. My aunt was a mercurial figure—in the space of a few minutes she could be autocratic or flirtatious, dismissive or charming. I loved her vivacity and the way she seemed to fill any room she entered, the way a full room seemed empty as soon as she left it.

But sometimes I was apprehensive around her, and occasionally felt chastened by an edgy comment or an imperious look she sent my way. During the months I lived with her in Scotland, she told me several times that she could read me like a book. I never really knew what she meant, but I hoped she was misreading whatever book she thought I was. As a twenty-one-year-old girl with a hidden past, the thought that anyone could see inside me was unnerving. Standing in front of an intimidating family member who claimed to be able to see right through me was downright terrifying.

I liked working in Scotland, perhaps because, in the United Kingdom, x-ray technicians are known as radiographers, a title I thought had much more class than our harsh-sounding North American term "technician." I also liked my new job because I could get lost in it. The Western Infirmary was a big raucous place, seemingly never quiet, even in the middle of the night. Situated near the banks of the Clyde River in the heart of Glasgow, this hospital served people from all corners of Scottish society and never seemed to run out of patients. Day and night they filled the halls and corridors. When at work, I always wore a little red maple leaf pin on my uniform: it not only signalled my Canadianness, but also functioned as a good conversation starter.

One night my maple leaf pin acted as a bit of a bodyguard. I happened to be on duty on New Year's Eve that year, or rather, Hogmanay as the Scots call it. Hogmanay is an important time in Scotland, filled with long-standing traditions. One of the most prominent traditions is known as "first-footing," referring to the luck that accompanies the first person to cross any threshold after midnight. The luck the "first-footer" brings into the household sets the tone for that family for the whole year. To ensure that happy times are on the way, many Scots celebrate Hogmanay vigorously, quite often too vigorously. By midnight I had lost track of the number of skull x-rays I had taken, and my lineup of patients still extended a long way down the radiography department's corridor. Some of the more inebriated ones were a little difficult to handle, even belligerent. Having learned that most Scottish people like Canadians, I began pointing to my little maple leaf whenever a patient with a bleeding head started to misbehave. His tone usually changed immediately: "Ach, here's a wee Canadian lass to take pictures of me broken head."

Working didn't take up all my time while I was in Scotland. In October that year, as Pierre Trudeau was invoking the War Measures Act back in Canada, I was travelling through the stunning Scottish Highlands on a fascinating road trip with one of my cousins. We saw beautiful islands, ancient castles, and herds of highland cattle as we sped up and down one-track roads under uncharacteristically clear blue skies.

One day, our car began to malfunction just after we picked up a charming Scottish hitchhiker. As we sputtered to a stop, he jumped out and said he knew what was wrong. He fiddled around under the "bonnet" for a few minutes, announced that he had fixed it, but that he had to take it for a test drive to make sure. As he disappeared in our car, with all our belongings and our purses, we looked at each other with wide eyes and rising panic. Minutes passed that felt like an hour. Just as we were trying to figure out how we would tell Big Daddy that we had given away the car, our hitchhiker returned. The pesky mechanical problem had disappeared. We thanked him profusely, delivered him to his destination as fast as we could, and carried on our way, picking up no more hitchhikers for the rest of the trip.

With another one of my cousins, I took the train to London for a weekend. We wandered through Soho and bought mod clothes on Carnaby Street, my memory of that experience now an indiscernible blur of colour and noise. We saw the controversial musical *Oh! Calcutta!* and decided that its dancing group nude scenes had an innocent quality whereas the clothed scenes were decidedly more sinister.

Back in Glasgow, I enjoyed a short flirtation with a Scottish doctor I met at work. I went to Edinburgh to see its famous castle, took in the sights along the Royal Mile, and gazed at the gothic-looking monument to Sir Walter Scott as I shopped my way down Princes Street. Scotland made an indelible imprint on my heart during my time there at the beginning of the seventies. I even toyed with the idea of staying for good.

But I was a little homesick. I received regular mail from Canada. My mother's newsy letters on tissue-thin, blue air-mail paper were not addressed to me, but to everyone in the household. We read them together in the evenings. Several other letters came addressed only to me: two from the handsome Canadian Forces pilot I had dated before I left Winnipeg. I kept those to myself.

I also received two short notes, my name scrawled across the envelopes in my father's almost illegible handwriting. The first was telling me not to get hijacked if I decided to fly anywhere. (Airline hijackings were prominent in the news those days.) The second was to tell me that our beloved black Labrador retriever had perished in a hunting accident. Years later, my brother told me the details. While fetching a downed bird, she had fallen through some thin ice and couldn't get out. My brother lay down on the ice and started to inch his body over the ice to rescue her. He heard and felt the ice cracking underneath him but kept going. Then he felt my father's hands around his ankles pulling him back. They could do nothing but watch her go down.

The following spring I returned to Canada, to the new family home in Calgary. Right away, I found a job at a city hospital. I bought a little blue Fiat sports car that I loved to take for long drives on sunny days, always with the top down, big dark sunglasses perched on my nose and a crocheted yellow cloche on my head to keep my hair out of my eyes. I should have been carefree, my life spanning out ahead of me optimistically. But, after my busy time in Scotland, I was a little lonely. I had no friends in Calgary, so I spent much time by myself, had much time to think.

One day that spring, I decided to go for a drive and steered my little car onto the highway going west to Banff. Once there, I wandered around town and then went for a walk up near Tunnel Mountain. That day, I sat for a while on the Hoodoos Trail overlooking the Bow River Valley, surrounded by those stirring sandstone pillars that stand like rigid ghosts among the pines. Suddenly I realized that it was my baby's third birthday. I tried to see his three-year-old face, but no image would come. That day, the strange emptiness I had felt hovering over me in the months after his birth returned, stronger than ever.

Much had changed in Canadian society in those three short years. Young people were actively challenging the rigid notions of sexuality and marriage. Around me, I saw more and more unmarried couples living together. Access to birth control information was readily available and many young unmarried women were on the birth control pill. Nevertheless, many unmarried young women still got pregnant. A startling difference was that now some of these girls kept their babies and became single mothers with the support of their families and their communities. I was stunned by these social shifts. Three years. That's what stood between me and my baby. Three years later and I never would have surrendered him, even if I'd had to do it alone. I didn't realize it at the time, but I had experienced first-hand an example of what happens when individual lives collide with their particular historical moments.

CHAPTER NINE

Motherhood and Me

AFTER I HAD BEEN back in Canada for a few months, the handsome pilot I had met before going to Scotland came west to visit me. While I was gone, the Canadian Armed Forces had moved him again, even farther east to a base in New Brunswick. This time he wanted me to go with him. Later that summer, on a glorious Alberta afternoon in downtown Calgary, with a modest gathering of family and friends smiling all around us, we got married. My aunt came over from Scotland to be part of the wedding fun. She stood in the front row of the church beside my parents. My mother wore a little yellow pillbox hat that sat neatly on the back of her head. My aunt wore a huge pink hat that blocked the view of anyone standing behind her.

The next day, as smiling newlyweds, we headed east. Driving my little blue Fiat all the way across Canada to the other end of the country, we talked and sang as the miles melted past. John Lennon's "Imagine" played often on the little car radio: "Imagine all the people, living life in peace . . ." I still see blue sky and highway when I hear those lyrics.

Living far away from my family in the Maritimes, my new husband and I tried to settle into our version of marriage, determined to figure out our own way of living our lives together. And we did, in the beginning. I definitely planned to find self-satisfaction in work outside my home. Having worked in hospitals in Winnipeg, Glasgow, and Calgary before my marriage, I knew I was a good x-ray technician and had no trouble finding a job in my new province. My most vivid memory from working at the hospital in Fredericton, New Brunswick, is from watching the small television in the staff room on my break one day and seeing Paul Henderson score the winning goal in the 1972 Summit Series between Canada and Russia. I swear that the whole hospital erupted in cheers.

My husband and I shared domestic duties, although I admit that might have been for practical reasons: I didn't really pay much attention to dust, didn't like to vacuum, and wasn't a very good cook. One night, I tried to make a meat loaf. I bought some ground beef, mixed it together with some chopped onions, added salt and pepper, and put it in the oven. An hour later, I pulled out a loaf pan filled with little pieces of onions and teeny round balls of grey-brown beef floating around in melted fat. While my new husband tried without success to stifle his laughter, I phoned my mother in a bit of a panic. She gave me improvised instructions about how to turn my failed meat loaf into the dinner I had known as the macaroni thing back when I was a kid in Winnipeg.

The week after my phone call home, a big envelope appeared in my mailbox. In it was a short note from my mother wrapped around a bundle of familiar recipes—including her oatmeal-enhanced meat loaf, the macaroni thing, and a tuna casserole. My parents liked my husband a lot and wanted him happy, so my mother also included directions about how to produce proven husband-pleasers like apple crisp and banana loaf.

Receiving that recipe package was the moment I discovered the truth about the "homemade" birthday cake we kids had all loved so much back when we lived in the house with the broken two. Apparently, our favourite cake was a store-bought mix and the icing was a recipe my mother found on the side of the box. My mother had enclosed a label from the mix box so I could find it in the grocery store. I liked that revelation—it was as if I had finally been let in on a big family secret. Secrets aren't quickly or easily relinquished in our family, and some are more difficult to uncover than others. With its satisfying secret and practical advice, that envelope of family recipes launched me on my own way to becoming an acceptable cook. Soon, I even decided to attempt a Sunday meal complete with roast beef, vegetables, and gravy. I didn't need recipes for those dishes because I had watched my mother make them for so many years. And I hadn't been surprised that my mother's gravy recipe was not among those in the recipe bundle—it's not something that can easily be written down.

After we had been married for about a year, I went to a doctor because I had been having a lot of headaches. He diagnosed them as migraines and strongly recommended that I stop taking my birth control pills. When I inquired about other means of contraception, he replied that it was about time I started having babies anyway. I smiled and said nothing, didn't protest. Indeed, one of my first thoughts after getting married had been that I could now legitimately have a baby. So we complied with my doctor's advice, and, less than a year later, our beautiful first daughter arrived.

She was born the day before Halloween, in the early evening, after a much different birth experience than my first one. My doctor checked in with me regularly. The nurses were kind and attentive. My husband was with me during early labour at home, then at the hospital, and even in the delivery room. Having fathers in the delivery room was a relatively new aspect of the birth experience those days, and the nurses weren't quite sure what to do with him. Being the curious type, he didn't want to miss anything. He kept moving around the room, and the nurses kept moving him back to his assigned spot beside my head.

Later that night, after the pain had abated and the excitement of her birth was settling into a contented calm, I held her close and tried unsuccessfully not to think about my lost child. Was he thriving? Was he loved? Did the woman who had become his mother feel about him the way I felt about this little bundle now sleeping in my arms? The ache was intense, but the only thing I could do was hold her tighter and put him in a safe inner place. It was around that time that I began talking to him in my mind: Be well, my son, be safe, be happy.

Over the coming years, I would occasionally think of hiring a private investigator to find him, but that seemed like something only people in movies or sensational novels did. I also felt that I had no right to look for him. I had given him away. I had signed those papers. I had no right to know anything about him. That was that.

My mother flew out from Calgary about a week after my

daughter's birth. She hadn't been in Eastern Canada since our family moved back west from Moncton in the fifties. I thought she would want to go back and visit her old neighbourhood, but my mother expressed no desire to see the small Maritime city she used to live in. In fact, she didn't want to go anywhere. New Brunswick's beautiful fall colours were on full display, but she was happy to see them only from our little house, so we didn't do any sightseeing at all the week she stayed with us. Instead, we stayed at home, passed my baby girl back and forth, took her for little walks up the street in her carriage, and watched over her as she slept in her bassinet. I think that was the best time I ever spent with my mother.

In the world outside my life, the turbulent sixties had given way to the tumultuous seventies. On the music scene, the fresh-faced Beatles had become a longhaired, guru-seeking, disillusioned band of arguing artists before finally splitting up. Elvis had so successfully resurrected his flagging career with such hits as "Don't Cry Daddy" and "In the Ghetto" that he was able to buy his own airplane. In world events, Pierre Trudeau still ran Canada, but Richard Nixon's US presidency was coming under increasing Watergate pressure. The Vietnam War raged on. The Irish Republican Army set off bombs in the Tower of London, and the Gay Liberation Front was becoming a worldwide organization.

Tucked away in that eastern corner of Canada, I was snug in my little life. The year after our daughter's birth was the best year of that marriage. We lived in a tiny little house with an orange shag rug on the living room floor. Our little girl was an easygoing baby with a gorgeous big smile. We lost ourselves in our magical child, and a cozy warmth settled over our lives. We had a wide circle of friends. Backyard barbecues were our favourite type of gathering. Fresh lobster was abundant. We'd have it on a Tuesday night sitting at a picnic table with our neighbours. I'd never had lobster before and couldn't get enough of its succulent texture. I rarely eat lobster anymore because nothing tastes like those ones, fresh from the ocean, their juices running down my face and arms, dripping onto my bare feet, a transistor radio playing in the background.

Happy as we were, I yearned for the day when we could move back west. Being a military family, we didn't have to wait long. A year and a half after our daughter was born, halfway through my next pregnancy, we moved again, from the Maritimes to Alberta, taking up residence in Edmonton, a city not unlike Winnipeg yet entirely new to me.

From the beginning, my third pregnancy was unusual. I was healthy enough, but this was unlike my other two, where I carried my babies fairly neatly and without too much discomfort. This time, my stomach was huge and I was very uncomfortable. I shared this information with my new Edmonton doctor, but he was unconcerned. He said I was fine. He said my baby was fine too, just quite large, at least ten pounds, maybe more. I should have asked more questions, pushed him harder to investigate, but my voice stayed silent.

More than a little apprehensive about the impending birth, I finally made it to the end of a long, difficult nine months: my husband was away on flight training in Ontario for the last weeks of my pregnancy, I had no friends to call on in my new home city, and my almost-two-year-old daughter was hard work for my very awkward body. My massive stomach ultimately restricted my wardrobe to one billowing yellow dress. I began to dream that my monster child would tear me apart making its entrance into this world.

During the last month, every time I went for my weekly checkup, my doctor suggested that he could induce labour. I resisted. Maybe out of fear, but also because I didn't think I should need to be induced. My other babies came on their own; why shouldn't this one? A week before my due date, my doctor insisted that enough was enough. My due date was probably wrong and I was two or three weeks overdue, he told me. He said he had no choice but to induce labour, and I no longer had the strength to protest.

Once again, as in 1968, I found myself alone in a dark labour room. I wasn't scared this time, but I was lonely and felt abandoned again. Nevertheless, after a thankfully short and relatively easy labour late one Friday night in November, the doctor held up my newborn infant for everyone in the delivery room to admire: a lean, screaming, red-faced baby boy weighing far less than ten pounds protested his arrival into a world of glaring lights and masks. Puzzled, my doctor took a second look into my birth canal: "Nurse," he said, "get another bassinet in here. We've got another one."

I barely had time to say "Another what?" or "I can't do that again right now," when four minutes later, my youngest daughter was born, bum first, not breathing. Chaos ensued. My infant son was whisked away. Medical staff appeared in droves out of nowhere, but I hardly noticed them. I couldn't take my eyes off the tiny white body in my doctor's hands as he gave her mouth-to-mouth resuscitation while the nurses ran around gathering equipment. Breathe, baby, breathe, I urged from my prone position too far away. And breathe she did. Only a little smaller than her brother, she weighed in at just under six pounds. Bonus baby, I said silently to her. You are my beautiful bonus baby.

Much later that night, at my insistence—I had to see that they were okay—the nurses reluctantly brought my babies to me even though they thought I should be resting. Together we admired my two sleeping infants. As I gazed at them, marvelling at how perfect they were, the nurses made their own observations. "Look at how their fingernails aren't quite formed," they said. "It's a good thing you refused to be induced because you weren't overdue at all," one nurse said. "They're one week early," said another. "Those babies needed these past three weeks to gain some weight," they said. The nurses looked at me with nodding admiration: "Mothers always know," they said. As I listened to them praise my so-called motherly wisdom, I couldn't help but think back seven years, back to a time when other nurses had dismissed me as an amoral nuisance. Now I was a source of innate maternal knowledge. But I was the same person: more experienced, yes, but the same person nonetheless.

The next morning, my doctor came in, shaking his head. "I don't know how I missed them," he said of my undiagnosed twins. He told me that I must have given him wrong information. Or held something back. Surely, there must be a history of twins in my family I didn't tell him about. Silently, I was doing some thinking of my own: together my twins' birth weight added up to almost twelve pounds, and I'm not a very big person, so I didn't know how he missed it either. Many pregnant friends of mine had had ultrasound tests. Why hadn't he ordered one for me? I thought these things, but said nothing out loud. I had discovered that about myself: often my voice strangled in my throat when I knew I should be speaking up. I didn't know why, but, at that particular moment in my life, I didn't have time to give my silence much further thought.

As the days and weeks went by, I was deluged with questions about my inability to know what was going on in my own body from almost everyone I called with my news. "What did having two babies inside you feel like?" several asked. "Better you than me," a few said.

The day after they were born, my mother came up from Calgary to see her new grandchildren. "How could you not have known?" she said, shaking her head at me. Unfortunately, we would have no quiet mother-daughter time after the birth of my twins. She was running a small card shop in Calgary and couldn't take time away from the business. She returned home the same day she came. I was on my own.

The nurses in the hospital were concerned that the father of my babies hadn't been up to visit us. They questioned me often as to when he was coming. I told them he was away. I could see that they didn't believe me. My room was filled with flowers from family and friends. The nurses asked me which ones were from my husband. A few days later, a social worker came to see me. She said that I would not be released from the hospital until I could show them I had enough help at home to cope. I told her that I wouldn't have any help for several more weeks, until after my husband got home. She shook her head, said that wasn't good enough. She handed me a brochure about homecare services. I went to the pay phone in the hospital lobby and called the number on the brochure. I hired an unknown housekeeper I had never seen and asked them to call the hospital to let them know so that my babies and I could be released.

When I finally brought my babies home from the hospital, my two-year-old daughter admired them for the first few hours before tiring of their attention-demanding presence: "Nice babies go home now, Mommy," she soon demanded. During the next few weeks, she learned that not only were those babies part of her home, but also that home had changed considerably.

Our new version of home was more than a little frantic for a long while. As a member of Canada's military, my husband was surrounded by a particularly rigid ideology of duty and performance that did not include family. In the seventies, a well-known old armed forces proverb was that if the generals and colonels wanted their men (and they were virtually all men in those days) to have wives and children, they would have distributed them along with the rations and the uniforms. When I suddenly became the mother of three on that unforgettable night in Edmonton, this proverb still reflected where my family stood on the military priority list. My husband was not scheduled to come home until he finished training in Ontario several weeks later and a schedule was a schedule. His squadron did send me flowers, which were very pretty, but, while I don't mean to sound ungrateful, if I couldn't have my husband with me, a second pair of hands for an afternoon or two would have been much more useful than a bunch of flowers.

Nevertheless, somehow, after being released from the hospital, we—my babies, my two-year-old, and I—got through each day and night, but not without some special help. The military community has its contradictions. Although no one from my husband's new squadron offered a hand, two friends from our old base in the Maritimes came through for me. I don't know what I would have done without either one of them. One, newly relocated to Edmonton herself, looked after my two-year-old daughter until the twins and I were released from the hospital. My other friend flew out from the Maritimes with her own nine-month-old to help me until my husband came home. The first thing she did was fire the housekeeper the homecare services had sent me, a large woman who liked to sit in my rocking chair holding my babies while I did the laundry.

When my husband finally arrived home several weeks after their birth, he was instantly enchanted with his expanded family. The next few years passed in a flash. Although he was away a lot, we managed pretty well. I knew we were lucky. Our children were healthy, and so were we. I felt special, blessed because I'd become a mother of three babies. I'd look at my three little ones and marvel at my good fortune. I have never told anyone this, but, deep inside myself, I felt as if I had been forgiven for surrendering my first child, as if some higher power had pardoned me for that mistake. But I hadn't forgiven me. And I hadn't forgotten.

I was also terrified of getting pregnant again. It seemed obvious to me that I was very fertile, that all we had to do was think about having sex and I'd be pregnant. I knew I couldn't handle any more at the moment. I began to think a little irrationally. If I got pregnant again, I was convinced I would have triplets. I talked to my doctor about my fears. A strong proponent of population control, he told me I had enough children already. In what I think was an attempt at humour, he said that he should just "yank out" my uterus, that it was a useless organ now anyway. Why I didn't tell him to yank out one of his own useless organs, I don't know. His serious suggestion was a tubal ligation. He said I could probably use a little break anyway. So, less than a year after my twins were born, he checked me into the hospital with the diagnosis "tired mother syndrome" and tied my fallopian tubes. No more fertility worries for me, he said. Just relax.

But relaxation was elusive for me. After a few years, our little family unit began to strain. My husband tried hard. When he was at home, he was involved, up to his elbows in diapers and laundry. But he wasn't home much, and, despite the souvenirs and gifts he brought me from every place he went, I started to resent the exotic life he seemed to live. Things grew tense between us. Jokes involving the word *divorce* were no longer funny. I tried not to worry. It'll pass, I said to myself, but I distanced myself from him, tried to silence the gnawing inside me, to bury the dissonant voices in my head.

Since mothering three toddlers became my primary function, the outside world grew more distant, and I became even more oblivious to it. I no longer heard the songs that played on the radio. I no longer noticed the news that flickered across the television screen. I no longer made time in my day to read a newspaper. I have often joked that the only thing I remember about the two years after my twins' birth was that Elvis died one August day shortly after my birthday. The news came over the radio and found its way into my consciousness. I stood stunned in my living room, taken instantly back to a dark movie theatre in Winnipeg where I had snuck in to see *Blue Hawaii* when I was twelve years old even though my mother had forbidden me to see it because it wasn't suitable for young girls. Now Elvis was dead and I was no longer a young girl.

As oblivious as I was to world events outside my family, I could not be oblivious to a subtle change that had happened in my immediate sphere. Although I threw myself into mothering with gusto, and genuinely enjoyed the experience of that most intimate love, I became aware that the aura around me had changed. I realized that, when socializing with adult friends and family, conversations involving me always ended up being about the children. When I talked to my parents on the phone, they asked me about the kids and then asked to talk to my husband so he could tell them about his latest trip.

This situation wasn't entirely the fault of the people around me: at that point, I don't think I had much to say about anything that wasn't related somehow to raising children. Nevertheless, I felt this subtle change keenly. The tangible shift in others' perceptions of who I was did not match my perception of myself. While I relished nurturing and talking about the three little people who had taken over my life, I gradually became aware that "Myrl" had disappeared, replaced in everyone's eyes but my own by "Mom."

I began to feel restless. Those around me tried to soothe my itch: "You're a good mother," they said. "You're doing the most important job in the world," they said. I would accept their comments with a small smile and silence. As satisfying as being mother to my children was, in my inner self I knew that something was missing from me: I was missing from me. The emptiness I had felt after the birth of my first son returned. I started having migraine headaches again.

My marriage floundered, gradually at first and then with a huge upheaval. I decided I needed a job and found one almost immediately. Then I rented a townhouse. The children and I moved out of our family home. My parents and siblings were horrified. Everyone in and around our lives urged me to go to marriage counselling. Together with my husband, I did just that. However, I soon realized that I was the one being counselled: for two-thirds of the counselling team—my husband and the counsellor—I was the one who needed fixing. It became clear to me that the goal of marriage counselling was not to help us reconcile our differences, but to rein in the restless female I had become. I resisted and shut down those counselling sessions soon after they began.

Friends and family warned me that I would be alone, that being a mother of three alone in the world was too scary for me. But I wasn't concerned about being alone: I had been alone before. When that didn't work, they told me I was being selfish. But I had been accused of being selfish before, back as a pregnant eighteen-year-old who mused out loud that she might keep her baby.

After several months of turmoil, much to the dismay of almost everyone around me, I decided that the split was final. Despite the sense that I was losing my "good" mother status and slipping into "bad" mother territory because of my so-called selfishness, I knew that I couldn't stay there. The marriage is finished, I said. And it was. I didn't see myself as selfish. Somehow, I knew that if I were unhappy in my life, my children would be unhappy, too. In retrospect, I have often wondered if ending my marriage was unconsciously rooted in a latent feminism I hadn't acknowledged. But I don't think it was. I was just a young woman who refused to stay in an unhappy marriage, refused to be an unhappy wife standing at a kitchen sink full of dirty dishes, releasing resentful sighs my children could hear.

My life was difficult for a while. Before arriving at work, I hurried to drop my daughter off at kindergarten, hurried to deliver the twins to daycare. After work, I hurried to pick them all up. In the evenings, I hurried to feed us all and do the laundry. The next morning, I hurried to get up early so I could do it all over again. I worked hard and made very little money. But I made new friends in my work and met someone who became an important friend. One night, my new friend and I danced together at a party. He was a very good dancer and during that dance I began to realize that we were going to be more than friends.

Our relationship deepened and soon I wanted to proceed with a divorce. I found a lawyer and told him that what I wanted most in my divorce was custody of my children. I told him that I wanted no alimony for myself, but that I wanted regular child support. I didn't expect large payments, just reasonable amounts within my husband's means. Today, ours would be a simple collaborative divorce, but, in 1980, collaborative negotiation and no-fault divorces were unheard of. The law assumed that a marriage breakup had to be somebody's fault and that all divorcing couples must be filled with animosity toward each other. To defend against that animosity, or perhaps to channel it as settlement leverage, or perhaps as a lawyer employment program, the legal system insisted that both sides of a divorcing couple had to have their own lawyers.

The legal system also had a waiting period for most divorces to become final at that time, a waiting period of several years. I didn't want to wait that long to get my divorce. Knowing that I was involved with someone new, my lawyer told me that I could get a divorce almost immediately if I admitted to adultery in court. He said the opposing lawyer would probably try to humiliate me a little bit, but that in the end everything would be fine. I told him I'd been humiliated in my life before, that the only thing that mattered to me in this divorce was having my children with me.

What I remember most about my day in the divorce court was that it was all so superficial and foolish. My lawyer told me to look good for the judge, so I obediently paid extra attention to my appearance that day. I wore a lovely white angora sweater and a tartan skirt. When I was called to the witness stand, I expected to be questioned about my mothering habits and had thought about what my answers would be, what I would say about managing three small children while holding down a paying job.

My husband's lawyer began by asking if I was the mother of the three children named in the petition. I said yes. Then he asked me if I had committed adultery. I said that I had. Then he asked me if I had committed adultery with a man or a woman. I said a man. With that, the judge said I could step down. Then he adjourned the proceedings. The whole thing lasted about three minutes. I was granted sole custody. My husband became my ex-husband. He and I went for a drink afterwards and had the best talk we'd had in a long time. I promised him that he would have generous access to the children, that he was an essential part of their lives. We've been good friends ever since. To this day, he is still part of my family.

For a long time afterwards, I often thought about those strange few minutes in that divorce court. I often wondered what the outcome would have been if my circumstances and my answers had been different, if I had admitted to adultery with a woman rather than a man. To me, the court had an odd way of measuring parenting skills. Not once did anyone ask me what kind of breakfasts I made for my children, how I disciplined them when they misbehaved, or what stories I read to them before they went to bed. All they wanted to know was the gender of the person I had sex with. So much for the state staying out of the nation's bedrooms.

Not long after my divorce was final, I married again. My new husband and I bought a little house in a mature neighbourhood in Edmonton. As my children settled into another new school, I promised my oldest daughter, who had changed schools several times in only three years, that the next time she had to change schools would be because she was finished with the one she was in. I wanted stability for my family. My ex-husband and my new husband helped the situation immensely by becoming friends with each other. When Christmas came along, my children never had to go from one parent's house to another. We simply all got together and still do.

I also wanted another child, one with my new husband, but I'd had that pesky tubal ligation. I'd heard that sometimes they were reversible, and I wanted to find out more. I went to a doctor recommended by a friend. She said he was very pleasant and seemed up on current medical treatments. On the day of my appointment, the doctor was courteous as he asked about my medical history and took notes as I answered. Things went well until I said that I wanted to investigate reversing my tubal ligation. He threw down his pen and said, "You women, always changing your minds. Can't you ever be happy?" I did not respond in words, as I should have. I just got up, walked out of his office, and never went back.

Before I went to another doctor, I did some investigation of my own and, fortunately for me, somehow ended up at the fertility clinic at the University of Alberta. There I began to see Dr. Joseph Scott, perhaps the kindest, most sincere medical practitioner I have ever met. Dr. Scott operated on me twice in his efforts to unblock my fallopian tubes. After the first operation, he said that the doctor who had "tied" my tubes was certainly determined I should never get pregnant again: he hadn't just tied them; he snipped the ends off, folded them up, and clamped them shut with big metal clips.

When I did not conceive after the first surgery, Dr. Scott thought he could still help me. He operated again, flushing my tubes out to make certain they were open. I had several painful follow-up treatments in his office in the months after the surgery to make certain they stayed open.

But, when over a year passed and I still wasn't pregnant, we knew that my reproductive system was not working as hoped. I think Dr. Scott was as upset as my husband and I were. Out of options he could offer us, Dr. Scott recommended in vitro fertilization. We considered it, but the procedure was very expensive, and we didn't have extra money at the time. We were also emotionally spent. After a while, I suggested that my husband and I adopt a child together. My husband reminded me that he had essentially adopted three children when we got married. He said he was content with our family the way it was. Later that year, we added a beautiful golden retriever puppy to our household.

Secretly, I hoped that once the stress of the surgeries and the treatments waned, I would still conceive, but that didn't happen. Having once been worried that I was too fertile, I now knew what it felt like to be infertile. I told myself to be grateful for the three children I had, and I was, and I am. Yet, while raising them, I never forgot that I had given birth to four. Birthmothers never forget. I still mourned the child I gave away. Now I had another child to mourn: the one I couldn't have.

CHAPTER TEN

Three Funerals

MY FATHER WAS one of the most sociable people I have ever known. He didn't like solitude. He liked to be with people, the more the better. He was happiest in the middle of a crowded party, in the stadium cheering for his Winnipeg Blue Bomber football team, on a curling rink surrounded by teammates, in a cold, damp duck blind with his hunting buddies and his son, in the backyard barbecuing for family and friends, in the kitchen with his five children clamouring to get at the brand new black Labrador puppy tucked inside his coat.

The only people I ever saw him uncomfortable with were my two grandfathers. My father always addressed my big burly maternal grandfather as "Sir" and was unusually quiet whenever he came to visit. Similarly, my father always deferred politely to his own father, always tending dutifully to his needs and comforts. By contrast, Dad was always a little playful with his mother, often gently teasing her. They had an impish bond, as if they were playful conspirators plotting to challenge the tide of wisdom that flowed without fail from my worldly grandfather.

Although he was born in Calgary, my father grew up in Winnipeg. Named after the beloved older brother my grandfather had lost in the aftermath of the Great War, my father was the only son, his parent's adored boy, his sister's cherished brother. She was the older, more sensible one; he was the antic-prone wild child.

A natural athlete as a boy, my father participated in few sports during his adult life. He was a very good curler. In the fifties, he was part of a team that made it to the Canadian Brier. For many years, he wore his pin-covered bonspiel sweater proudly. Until one of my sisters recently reminded me, I had forgotten that in his later years, Dad also enjoyed golf. She remembers cringing as she watched him leave the house for the golf course wearing one of his garishly patterned shirts and a pair of loud plaid pants. Now she thinks of those outfits as his happy clothes.

Although blessed with a clever mind, my father chose not to pursue further education after high school. His affability made him a natural salesman. He spent most of his working years selling various commodities such as building products or heavy-duty farm equipment. He enjoyed meeting people, but his work had consequences. The constant travel, the unstable levels of income, the socializing that salesmanship demands—that he so easily gave himself up to—all contributed to stress at home. As children, we sensed the onset of uneasy times, held our breath in the dark periods, and basked during some glorious happy days. As a parent, my father was often absent when he should have been home—and was often absent even when he was at home. Nevertheless, somehow we kids always knew that our father loved us. And we loved him back.

I was always relieved when my father finally arrived home in the evenings, even if I knew my mother was angry with him. I knew that, after some strained conversation, my mother's mood would eventually soften as a small smile chased the frown from her face. Then she would join him for a drink, sit with him at the kitchen table while he ate his late dinner, linger with him there as they chatted about the day's events. That's when we kids breathed a little easier, ambled in to give them each a kiss at bedtime, then fell asleep to the comforting sound of their voices talking quietly into the night.

He had a terrific singing voice, deep and soothing, so different from the thunder of the raised voice that sometimes woke me up during my parents' arguments. On weekend mornings, he used to sing as he shuffled around the kitchen wearing slippers and his old brown bathrobe: "Hello, Dolly" or "Ramblin' Rose" or "I Was Dancin' with My Darlin' to the Tennessee Waltz." I used to lie longer in bed just to listen to him croon as he tossed ingredients into the blender for his special scrambled eggs. I could picture him cracking the shells with his nicotine-stained fingers, tossing in chopped green onions and lots of blue cheese. I could hear my mother working beside him, making the toast, frying up the bacon, laughing as he switched from song to song.

My parents had an active weekend social life. Sometimes, after an evening out on a Saturday night, they brought their friends back to our house, and my father would turn on the small high fidelity phonograph that sat in the corner of the living room. He always played the same record. Not the soothing sounds of his mellow morning croonings, this was march music: "When the Saints Go Marching In" or "The Yellow Rose of Texas" or "Seventy-Six Trombones." Lying awake upstairs, we waited for our cue. Soon my father's voice boomed it out: "Has anyone ever seen my kids march?" In an imperfect parade line, we would file downstairs and circle the room several times, knees stepping high, hands imitating trombone movements, while my father played band leader and my mother tried to chase us back up to bed.

As the years passed, my father didn't like the idea that we were growing up on him. He would have preferred that we remain children. He once told me to enjoy my high school days because afterwards life just wasn't as much fun anymore. I didn't know enough about life yet to be worried about such a remark.

One rainy night shortly after my sixteenth birthday, my father decided to teach me how to drive. I didn't particularly want to go, but he insisted. The rain pelted on the windshield as I manoeuvred the car awkwardly around the side streets of our neighbourhood. Afterwards, I thought I had done quite well and said so. He answered that I had done okay for a girl, but that boys were naturally better drivers. Then he told me I should prepare to be disappointed because I would probably fail my driver's test several times.

Months later, when I passed my driver's test on the first attempt, I waited impatiently for my father to arrive home that evening. As soon as he walked in the door, I proudly showed him my licence. His response was cranky: "Just because you have a licence doesn't mean you know how to drive." I was deeply hurt. But I eventually came to understand that he was worried that night. He didn't want me driving around by myself in what he had begun to see as an increasingly menacing world.

He always told me that I could do anything I wanted, meaning that I was capable of doing many things. Nevertheless, my father's expectations for his daughters' lives were definitely traditional: marriage and motherhood. When I became pregnant at age eighteen, his silence was deafening to my ears. Yet, it was his very silence that told me how distraught he was about my situation. Although he kept his innermost concerns to himself, I am convinced that, over the years, he must have thought at least occasionally, and probably more often than anyone will ever know, about the little boy our family had relinquished.

When I married and had children, he was proud. When my first marriage floundered, he was very unhappy with me. He urged me to go home and be a good wife. I didn't do that, but when I married again, my father welcomed my new husband graciously.

By the mid-eighties, our family had changed a lot since we lived in Winnipeg, back in the house with the broken two. We were scattered all across Western Canada. Mom and Dad lived by themselves in their South Calgary home. Only my brother and one of my sisters still lived in the same city as my parents: two sisters had moved to British Columbia. I was still in Edmonton.

In addition to living in a house with no children around them for the first time since the year after they got married, my parents' lives had changed in other ways. Whenever I saw them together, I felt the distance between them: they were together, yet not together; in the same room, but not in the same space. I know that long-married couples can often communicate without words and be quite content, but that's not what had happened to my parents. To one, the other seemed to have become invisible. They talked around each other, not to each other. I had no way of knowing whether they talked at all when they were alone. I feared not.

Occasionally, all of us gathered in Calgary for a Sunday dinner at my parents' house. The menu was still roast beef. My grandparents often joined us. As they grew older, my grandparents travelled less and less, finally limiting themselves to an annual visit to Scotland to see my aunt and her family. Most of the time, they stayed close to their Calgary home. Sunday dinner at my parents' house had become a big night out for them.

Gramp always sat in my father's big green chair and Granny perched on a corner of the sofa as they waited for their pre-dinner cocktails: scotch for him, gin and tonic for her. Gramp always wore a suit and tie; Granny always wore a good day dress, usually with her pearl necklace. She was never without her two favourite rings, on her left hand an unusual, square art-deco-style diamond, on her right a shamrock-shaped cluster of pearls.

I will always remember those visits because that's when I first saw Granny react to our babies, her great-grandchildren. As we proudly introduced her to each new arrival, she would gaze at the tiny bundle as if nothing like it had ever existed on this earth before. Unfailingly, each new babe rewarded her with a smile. Granny's first view of one of my nieces carried her for days. Dropping in for a short visit on my way out of town the day afterwards, I found her still smiling: "All I have to do is close my eyes, and I can still see that baby."

One day, I don't remember exactly when, in one of those few moments when my father and I were alone together, his voice grew quiet as he said, "You know, years ago I thought I had lost you." I knew what he was talking about, knew he was thinking about his first grandchild, knew that he was suggesting we could finally share our thoughts about that painful episode. But he caught me by surprise. It felt too sudden, too out of the blue. I panicked a little inside, so I said simply, "You didn't lose me, Dad. I'm right here." To my deep regret, the opportunity for that conversation never came again. I didn't know how little time we had left.

My grandparents remained relatively healthy. Their lives progressed in an easy, sedentary flow as they aged from their seventies into their eighties. It almost seemed as if they would live forever. What could possibly stop them from waking up each day?

Then came the years of fading strength, of two alert minds trapped in failing bodies, of seeing them go from living independently in their warm apartment to an assisted-living complex and finally to a full-care nursing home: two beds, side by side, filling a sparsely furnished room just off a busy institutional hallway. The staff was kind and treated them well. As the only married couple in the home, they achieved a certain status: a Mr. and Mrs. sleeping their days away between meals and visitors.

By this time, their worldly treasures were all gone. Possessions had become a burden and treasures had been mistaken for possessions. During the dispersal process, a family rift developed; communications between the Canadian and Scottish branches of our family grew tense, tangled, then firmly tightened into rigid knots. The foundation of the conflict was sorrow, but the outlet was anger. *Big Chief* and Lotso disappeared, lost to local art auctions. One of my sisters tried to save Lotso, but it was too late; he was gone.

Other than a few small photos, the walls in my grandparents' room at the nursing home were bare. Nevertheless, their institutional life settled into a routine they seemed to adapt to. My siblings and I visited, probably not often enough. My mother went several times a week. My father went every day, picking up their mail and delivering the morning newspapers to my grandfather.

At that point in our lives, I only saw my father a few times each year. We lived in different cities. I had my family and a full-time job to keep me busy; he seldom strayed far from home. During a short visit in what would be his last full summer, I was startled by his appearance. Always robust, he suddenly looked older than his almost sixty years. He had lost a lot of weight. His skin sagged on his body. His face looked blotchy, sallow, and tired. When I asked my mother what was wrong with him, she said he was fine. I didn't push her for more.

In his last years, my father's alcohol consumption had increased dramatically. My father had been a drinker as long as I could remember. Dad's workdays always ended with a drink (or two). His weekends began and ended with a drink. He wrapped up his Saturday chores with a drink. He watched his Sunday afternoon football with a drink. Back in our Winnipeg days, he seemed to have his relationship with alcohol under control: he could take it or leave it, even though he did more taking than leaving. I can remember him going "on the wagon" annually, usually after the Christmas holidays. One wagon trip lasted almost a year. My mother once told me that my father's year-long stay on the wagon was a good one for them.

But in the last decade of his life, he lost sight of that wagon and the alcohol took over. I don't know why, but I do know the consequences. He lost his job. He spent time in detoxification institutions. His stays there had little long-term effect; he simply charmed the doctors and nursing staff until he had convinced them that he could handle himself back in his world. Once released, he would be a little better for a short while, but he always drank again. With each relapse, his alcohol intake increased.

Family gatherings on Sundays and special occasions had become somewhat tense. My father had always seemed to take great joy in holiday festivities, but in the last years of his life he didn't seem to find much joy in anything. A year and a half before his death, fifteen family members all gathered in Calgary for Christmas. We were nervous. Would he fill his glass over and over again? Would Christmas revolve around a frightening, too-loud, false gaiety none of us could maintain?

Surprisingly, our worries were for naught. We had two-and-a-half days of calm. Slowly we all began to relax and enjoy the season, each other, and our memories. Many conversations began with "Remember the year we opened all the presents before Mom and Dad got up . . ." We raised our glasses in toasts and my father joined in, allowed himself a short drink or two, but no more. We ate and drank, laughed and played games. And then it was over.

The next Christmas was bleak. Immediately afterwards, before we could even ring in the New Year, my parents separated. They had been together for over thirty-five years. My mother moved out of the family home, leaving Dad alone in the house until it sold a few months later. After that, he moved into an apartment I never saw. Over the years, I have unsuccessfully tried not to imagine its bleakness.

Throughout all this, I told myself he would be okay. He had been through tough patches before: he survived a critical diving accident when he was a teenager and a brain aneurysm at age forty-seven. I kept telling myself that he would find a way to get through this, too.

During this time, my parents both continued their regular visits to see my grandparents in the nursing home, although I think my mother reduced hers to once a week. Then one day, nearly six months after my parents separated, my grandfather telephoned my mother to say that my father hadn't made his morning visit for several days. She knew immediately that something was wrong and sent one of his friends to the apartment he had moved into.

I didn't know any of this on the morning of that brilliant July day as I packed up our car. That afternoon, I enjoyed a splendid drive through the mountains with my husband and children. Around dinnertime, we pulled into the driveway of my sister's home in the Okanagan Valley, our first stop on a two-week holiday. A few minutes after we arrived, my sister pulled me aside and quietly told me that our father had been found dead in his apartment, slumped on the floor in front of the television. Her words had a physical impact I can still feel. It was as if I had slammed into a mountain.

That night I lay thinking about the last time I saw my father: I had walked away from him in anger that day. I thought about the last time I had heard his voice. He called me one night, and I knew immediately that he had been drinking. The phone call ended badly with me barely responding to whatever he said.

The next week is a blur of vague recollections punctuated by indelible memories. In the shock that was his funeral, I can clearly recall only a few moments. Those feel permanently freeze-framed in my head.

I remember the sight of my grandparents slumped side by side in their wheelchairs parked right beside my father's coffin at the front of the church.

I remember wearing my favourite yellow jacket, an odd choice for a funeral but my father never liked to see any of his daughters wearing black. He thought black was too sombre for young girls, and I knew that his four daughters would always be young girls to him.

I remember someone handing me a flower plucked from his casket just before it was loaded into the hearse. I had a stranglehold on that blossom for the rest of the day until it finally disintegrated in my hands.

I remember that I almost jumped out of my shoes when the funeral home attendants accidentally slammed the hearse door after sliding my father's casket inside. It sounded like a gunshot.

I remember that the actual funeral was generic and impersonal: perfunctory. No picture of my father adorned the program or gazed out at us from the front of the church. The service consisted of intoned Anglican prayers that my father would have been completely unfamiliar with. In his brief comments, the minister talked obliquely about not judging the life lived but being grateful that there had been a life at all. There was no eulogy, no personal tributes: no friends stood up to relate nostalgic anecdotes, no one from the family rose to say what he had meant to us.

To be fair to us, we didn't yet know that we would ache for him, that we would never stop listening for his voice. In that moment, we were all paralyzed by the suddenness of what we should have seen coming. But now I realize that saying nothing that day wasn't fair to him because he was so much more during his lifetime than his death suggests.

At the reception after his funeral, family friends talked quietly to my mother and each one of us before drifting away. I was standing nearby when someone offered condolences to my grandfather. Gramp didn't notice me as he responded: "Yes, my son had a difficult time. He could never live up to my accomplishments." I slipped further away so my grandfather wouldn't realize that I had heard him. In that moment, I understood more clearly what my father's life had been like. My grandfather had provided very well for his family. But he basked in the glow of his own self-esteem without realizing how it burned those closest to him. I'm not saying my grandfather caused my father's problems. My father would be the first to reject that theory. He made his own choices in life, and he would never have chosen not to be his father's son.

After a few hours, only the family remained at the funeral reception. My aunt, who had raced over from Scotland to attend the service, hovered over my grandparents as they sat waiting for their ride back to their nursing home. They looked shell-shocked. I felt so sad for them. They had seen my father every day. In fact, his regular morning visit may have been the highlight of their day. I mused out loud, unthinkingly, in a manner I sometimes lapse into that doesn't register all the implications of an ill-formed thought: "I think perhaps Granny and Gramp will miss him the most." My aunt drew herself up and threw a hard look at me and my siblings as she said, "I don't know about you lot, but I'm going to miss him very much." I didn't see her for four years after that.

I went back to my life, but my father haunted me. In a city he hardly ever visited, I often thought I saw him walking down the street, any street. I saw the shape of his head, his broad square shoulders, his familiar gait. Each time this happened, I had to pull my car over and let my heart stop racing. Madonna had released a song earlier that year called "Papa Don't Preach" about a young girl explaining to her father that she was keeping her baby and she needed him to be strong for her. Every time it came on the radio, I turned it off.

It wasn't only the unresolved conversations that I never had with my father that tormented me. Although I know now that the physical symptoms I noticed in that last year of his life are those of advanced liver disease, and although I know now that at that point he probably could not have been saved, that he had to have saved himself years earlier, and although I know now that adult children of alcoholics often have a tendency to hold themselves responsible for things beyond their control, I felt that I should have been able to save my father.

I was distraught that we didn't know the cause of his death. I needed a real, concrete, official, medical reason for him to be dead. My mother said the autopsy results were inconclusive. She suggested that he'd had a heart attack, but I knew that was unlikely: his heart was strong. Through one of my cousins, I learned that our Scottish family thought his death was related to his youthful diving accident and subsequent brain aneurysm: a plausible explanation, but I knew that it conveniently ignored the alcohol factor.

Eventually I decided that he died from despair, from a broken life. I began to think of his death as a passive suicide. With his doctor's warning that even one more drink could be fatal echoing somewhere in the background, I visualized him pouring one anyway. I saw him stand alone in a sparsely furnished apartment with a small television in the corner, a messy pile of newspapers scattered on the floor, the worn armchair from the basement of our old house facing the television, one of our flimsy folding metal tables probably standing beside it holding an overflowing ashtray. I saw him reach for a half-empty bottle of rye. I saw him settle into his chair and raise the glass to his lips, the silence in his room shouting at him. I could never get to the part where I saw him slide out of his chair onto the floor. A few years passed with me playing out that scene over and over in my head, at first daily, then weekly, eventually only once a month or so.

Three summers later, my sisters rented a cabin on the shores of Okanagan Lake, and the family gathered to spend a few days together. One morning, I lay half-awake in bed listening for sounds of movement, enjoying the feeling of having my whole family close by. I don't remember whether my eyes were open or closed and it doesn't matter, because suddenly I felt my father fill the room. Then I saw him standing in the corner. Then I heard his voice one last time: "It's okay. I'm okay." In that instant, a peace settled around my heart. Since that day, I've learned that grief becomes a strangely comforting part of existence. I miss him still, but missing my father is now simply part of me, part of who I am.

Four years after my father's death, my grandmother celebrated her ninety-second birthday. Dressed in an emerald-green jacket with a wilted silk flower on its lapel, she had many visitors that day. My grandfather commented that she was the most popular resident in the nursing home. I sat beside her as he entertained their visitors with stories I had heard many times before. Granny was particularly quiet that day and I asked her why. Her reply was succinct: "He's always talking. I can never get a word in." Her words had a little bit of an edge to them, something we rarely heard from Granny about Gramp. His response was a mere pause between sentences. Married seventy years, they had probably been through private moments like this many times. I reminded Granny that it was July, her month to celebrate: today her birthday, next week their wedding anniversary. "Yes," she said quietly, "if I live that long." She did live that long, but not much longer.

She fell sick that October. I remember the day I went to visit her in the hospital. I hadn't seen her since her birthday. Her skin had become so transparent I felt as if I was looking right at her bones. Her cheeks had withered to virtually nothing, but her jaws, both upper and lower, seemed enormous. The rest of her had almost disappeared. I was stunned to see how small she looked under the white hospital sheets. She had never been very big, but I didn't know how she suddenly got to be so small. Her younger self used to have plump little arms and a plump little chin; her cheeks used to be full, not hollow. Now she looked like a skeleton with skin.

As I sat in a chair beside her hospital bed, Granny lay quietly next to me, a tube in her nose, a drip in her arm, and tears in her eyes. She didn't try to speak. Holding her hand, I looked around the room, looking for something I could do for her, looking for anything to say, looking for Lotso. I could think of no words, so I just sat there holding her hand. I gazed out the window, watched gold and yellow leaves drift down to the ground. A few days later, she was gone. For the first time in seventy years, my grandmother left my grandfather behind instead of the other way around. For the first time in his life, he didn't know what to do.

Standing outside the church after her funeral service, we watched as the men in black put her into the back of the hearse, watched as it drove her away, watched as it disappeared down the street, tires crunching on dry autumn leaves. We watched as a fractured family: my mother, my brother, my sisters and me, my aunt from Scotland, my ninety-six-year-old grandfather sitting perfectly still in his wheelchair, and my father's ghost hovering over us all.

After the funeral, my aunt gathered up Granny's personal effects and returned to Scotland as soon as she could. The rest of us returned to our lives once again. Fall slid gently into winter that year, the November days fading into December. On Christmas afternoon, we gathered at the nursing home, arms full of candy and shortbread for my grandfather. He was still in their room, but it looked even more barren now. Her bed was gone, but nothing filled the gap it left. As we formed a semicircle around my grandfather's bed, no one set foot in the empty space where hers had been.

Lying fully dressed on top of the blankets, Gramp began to tell us a story, a new story, one we had never heard before. He was moving, leaving Canada to live in Scotland. Stunned and worried, we protested. In that moment, we felt that our Scottish family must be pressuring him unreasonably, but now I know that we were being a little unfair to them. Naturally, they wanted him to come to them, and naturally, he wanted to go. Although upset that he might not survive the trip, when my eyes fell on the spot where Granny's bed used to be, I knew that he had to get out of that room.

I tried to lighten the conversation. I told my grandfather how vividly I remembered skating with him on Sunday afternoons back in Winnipeg. "Yes," he said, "until you cried and said you wanted to go home." That part I hadn't remembered.

When we left that day, I knew I would never see him again. He did survive the trip, but lived only two months longer. He died in Scotland, in a nursing home on the banks of Loch Lomond, surrounded by his Scottish family. A few months later, my aunt brought his ashes back to Canada. Apparently there was a small funeral service, but I didn't go. It was enough for me to know that my grandparents are together again, in a cemetery in Lethbridge, Alberta, the city where my grandmother was born.

Several years passed with little contact between the Canadian and Scottish branches of our family. I fostered a small reconciliation by taking my eldest daughter over to visit them, and my cousins welcomed us enthusiastically. We didn't see much of my aunt and uncle. When we did, they were warm, but distant; polite, but reserved. After that trip, I never saw them either of them again. My uncle died first, followed a few years later by my aunt.

While tending to the sad chore of handling their mother's estate, my cousins had found the two rings that Granny always wore. During a subsequent trip that my eldest cousin and her husband made to Canada, I noticed that she was wearing one of Granny's rings. Before I could say anything, she handed me a small parcel. She had brought the other one as well, for me. I was delighted to have the ring, but even more delighted with the gesture and my cousin's comment that Granny would have wanted one of her favourite rings to be on the Canadian side of the Atlantic Ocean.

My grandfather's story has been well documented. He appears in official records and newspaper articles. His years as head of the Canadian Wheat Board have been shaped into a book based on hours of interviews the author taped as my grandfather told his stories. He is even on the Internet. He would be pleased about that, even though he would have no idea what it is. One day, in full-blown procrastination mode, I did a Google search for my grandfather expecting no results at all. Up popped a link to a short biography of him on the Manitoba Historical Society's website. One paragraph long, it ends by saying that he died while in Scotland on a holiday. I briefly wondered if I should correct them: he wasn't on vacation. He had left Canada for good.

My grandmother also appears occasionally in these records, sometimes by name, most often praised anonymously as his supportive wife, her story subsumed into his. That would probably be fine with her. She wasn't a big talker. In public, my grandmother was gracious and genteel: if she had negative thoughts, she kept them to herself. In private, she could be magnanimous and open.

Her family knew that she could also be stubborn and sometimes more than a little grumpy. For her granddaughters, she was a traditional role model, not an intrepid one. I don't think of her as having a tough spirit of adventure.

But even as I say that, I remember hearing a story about Granny loading her two small children into her car to drive from Winnipeg to Lethbridge so they could visit her sisters while my grandfather was far away. A journey that seems unremarkable today, in the 1930s when the Trans-Canada highway was non-existent, when two ruts in the endless landscape formed the prairie highway for long stretches, when modern service stations had yet to be invented, and when many women didn't drive at all, much less travel alone without male accompaniment, my grandmother's eleven-hundred-kilometre trek would probably qualify as an intrepid adventure taken by someone tough in spirit, although it would be one of those routine adventures that usually goes unrecorded and is lost in time.

CHAPTER ELEVEN

Questions without Answers

A FEW YEARS AGO, my brother told me a story I hadn't heard before, a story that dated back to when we were living in Winnipeg, in the house with the broken two. Most Sunday mornings, my mother took us to church with her. We usually went reluctantly, casting doleful glances back toward the house as we drove away. My father never went to church. He stayed at home, relaxing in his pyjamas and bathrobe, often getting brunch ready for us to eat when we returned.

My mother belonged to a local Anglican parish where it was customary for the children to accompany their parents in the main part of the church for the opening hymn and the early prayers. During the next hymn, all the children would parade out and go downstairs to their Sunday school classes in the basement. I liked that. Not because I was so eager to go to Sunday school, but I liked it better than staying upstairs for the whole service. I had done that once or twice. I didn't mind the hymn singing, or even the sermon. What I didn't like was all the sinning I was supposed to repent. It didn't make any sense to me. I was just a kid. I hadn't done anything wrong that I knew of. So I was happy to go down to my Sunday school class where we listened to stories and worked on art projects.

One Sunday, as my siblings and I rose to join the children's parade, my mother held my brother back. She said nothing, just made him sit with her upstairs all the way through the service. My brother was not a child who could sit still or keep quiet easily, but that Sunday morning he had to. Afterwards, he asked my mother why. She told him that his Sunday school teacher had complained that he asked too many questions during her class. My mother said nothing more about the matter, and the next week my brother was allowed to go back to his Sunday school class as usual. After he finished telling me this story, my brother commented that he never asked another question in Sunday school again.

So many of us (and by us I mean me and anyone else from a stereotypical North American family, if indeed such an entity exists) don't think about our surroundings when we are children. We grow up in our particular environments not knowing that we can ask questions about that environment. At least, that's what it was like in our family. My parents didn't readily share information with their children. We sometimes overheard them talking about family members or community affairs, but we weren't part of the conversation. And we definitely weren't encouraged to ask questions. As a result, we became good listeners but not good questioners. Sometimes we blurted out our questions anyway. We usually directed them at my mother because she was at home more than my father. This was unfortunate for her because my mother doesn't like questions.

Nevertheless, my mother easily answered some of the questions my siblings and I asked her, such as where did you go to school, what was your dog's name, or what was our dead grandmother like. But she deflected any questions we asked about my father and her, such as where did you meet, how long did you two date, where did you get married, why are there no pictures of your wedding, or how come you and Dad don't celebrate your anniversary like our friends' parents do. Those questions made her uncomfortable. When faced with them, she was stubbornly reluctant to provide anything more than terse replies usually in the form of a reinforced demand not to ask so many questions. The official story of their wedding was that my mother and father decided to elope because my mother's family had put on a big ceremony and reception for her sister just before my parents decided to get married. But that's as much as my mother would ever say. If he was at home, my father wasn't much better on the topic. He usually left the room or turned up the television.

In the last decade of the twentieth century, with a thriving family at a stage that finally allowed me more time for myself, I had questions. My life was good, very good, but I was not without my struggles. For one thing, I was having some difficulty finding a sustained career direction. My work as an x-ray technician had come to an end before my eldest daughter was born. More recently, I had worked with my husband for a few years in the business we began together. Our collaboration was good for business, but not for our marriage, so I left.

Luckily for me, I had never stopped being a student of sorts. I had always had an interest in photography and completed many evening courses in that medium. Those courses turned into a career opportunity when a film producer hired me as a stills photographer, and I came to spend several years working in the Alberta motion picture industry.

Between film jobs, I tended to my family and tried to solve my personal anxieties. I had developed a gnawing in my gut that just wouldn't go away. Almost ten years had passed since my father's death. I had come through those difficult first years but still found myself subject to dark times, as if falling into a pit. When this happened, I tried to keep my pit-falling to myself, but sometimes I erupted unexpectedly, as if there were no room left inside me for all the stuff I had pushed down there.

Never one to cry easily, I occasionally found myself dealing with a spontaneous outburst of huge body-shaking sobs. Fortunately, I was usually alone when this happened. In public, I maintained a calm front and kept a close rein on my emotions in case any runaway feelings might leak out. One night, at a gathering of girlfriends, someone I thought of as a close friend told me that what she liked most about me was that I didn't need anyone. I was deeply hurt, stunned to think that was how others saw me.

Yet, while at times I felt too much, at other times I still felt as if a part of me was somehow disengaged or stuck, anaesthetized or immobilized. This odd numbness contrasted with powerful waves of emotion that often swept over me, surges of love for everyone in my sphere, bouts of yearning for those who weren't there but should have been. I did not know how to reconcile these disparate parts of my being.

Looking for some remedy, I started seeing a psychologist. I was too embarrassed about my inner turmoil to ask my doctor for a referral, so I found one on my own by going through the yellow pages in the phone book. I felt I knew what I was looking for: I wanted to talk to someone about me. The psychologist I finally chose was one of the few listed who wasn't specializing in couple's counselling or anger issues or alcoholism. Her small ad said that her services focused on individual therapy.

When I called her office, she answered the phone herself. Her friendly voice drew me in. A few days later, I went to meet her. Located in the basement of her house, her office consisted of two rooms painted in soft colours, filled with big over-stuffed chairs and soothing music coming from an unseen source. She seemed to work entirely alone. After a short welcome, she asked me to start talking about anything that came to mind. So I did. I had been a little nervous about the whole thing, but once I started talking, the words flowed out almost non-stop.

For several months, for one hour a week, I talked. In fact, the thing I liked the most about that experience was being able to talk about myself for a whole hour and have someone just listen. Of course, my psychologist did more than that. She also gave me things to do between our sessions. One assignment was to take myself on a date. I spent an afternoon at the art gallery. Another assignment was to write for fifteen minutes every morning as soon as I got out of bed. This became part of my daily routine for about six months. The last assignment she gave me was to write a letter to someone I needed to talk to: your father or your mother, she said. I didn't like that idea. "What's the worst that can happen?" she asked. I had no answer for that question, but I still didn't want to write either of those letters.

"Fine," she said, looking across her teacup at me. "Then write a letter to the eighteen-year-old girl you used to be."

My letter to myself was short, but surprisingly easy to write: *Okay, so you screwed up. Don't over-analyze yourself. Possibly you were just looking for a little affection. Contrary to popular opinion, you do not lack moral character. You are not a bad person. Your life is not ruined. Yes, you were curious, but the great big sex act beckoned irresistibly as a way to fill a void you won't understand for years, may never completely understand. So give yourself a break sooner rather than later. The system is flawed, not you. Curiosity about sex is healthy. Unfortunately, according to the world you live in, not for girls. And you're right, it's not fair. But, as your future ex-husband likes to say, no one ever said life was going to be fair. As for your baby, don't believe a word of what they tell you. You will never forget. You will never stop thinking about him. But you will learn how to put him in a safe place in your heart and move on. Realize that the biggest issue you will have is that no one will let you talk about it. No one wants to hear your story. So you are going to bury it for a very long time. You will be fine.*

At the beginning of my regular session the following week, I pulled out my letter, ready to hand over my completed homework. I was surprised that my psychologist didn't want to read it. Instead, she asked me to tell her how I felt about it. "Better," I said, "different somehow." She asked me to describe that difference. I told her that something inside me seemed to have shifted, the empty feeling had faded, and the gnawing in my gut was gone. She said, "That's terrific. I think we're done." "Until next week," I responded. "No," she said, "I think we've done what we can do. Call me if you ever need to talk again." Taken aback, all I could say was thank you. When I left her office that day, I felt as if I had been fired. On the way home, the gnawing in my gut came back.

I never went to another psychologist, but I did keep writing. Soon a series of notebooks with intense bursts of personal reflections and anecdotes piled up in a corner of my office at home. After a while, my morning journal writing sessions started to branch out into other experimental forms. I produced some awkward, clunky poems, all about me, of course. I threw most of them out, but I kept one of them, the one I wrote for my lost son, imagining what I would say if I could have just one conversation with him:

> If I could talk with you but once,
> I would speak of youthful love and curiosity
> with no hint of blame or shame.
> If I could talk with you but once,
> I wouldn't waste a minute.
> I'd tell you our stories:
> the sadness in a young father's eyes,
> a brother by half denied a brother
> and sisters that light up the world.
> If I could look at you but once,
> I would tell you

about the shape of your chin or
the raise of your brow,
all the while not taking my eyes from your face.
Are they blue like mine or brown like his?
They were closed that last time late in the night.
I would tell you of the secret place
I have kept you all these years.
Safe. Warm. Loved.
Tucked away in the yellowed envelope
with that picture and those wristbands.
For to see you anywhere else was
unthinkable, not survivable.
And then I would pause because,
most of all, I need you to know,
somehow I would sort out how to say this—
I would not change that I gave you life,
but change I would the life I gave you.
If I could talk to you but once.

I thought it was a strange poem. I hadn't stopped moving my
pen even once as the words spread out on the page. The lines had
appeared in my head, and all I had to do was write them down.
After I tweaked some of the words around a little, I didn't know
what to do with it. I didn't want to crumple it up and toss it in the
wastebasket with the others. But I didn't want to send it out for
anyone else to read. I let it sit for a few days, then looked at it again.
I decided that it was self-indulgent crap. So I stashed it in a file of
old scribblings that I kept in the deepest corner of my desk.

Around this time, I had a disagreement with my mother—a big one. Not once since 1968 when she came to see me in the hospital after my first child was born had my mother and I talked about that part of my life.

After my sessions with the psychologist, I had come to realize that, next to not knowing where my son was or how he was doing, the hardest thing about my adoption experience was enduring the years of silence that had followed it. In addition to the two men I married, I had confided in only one or two close friends over the years. I had eventually told my sisters some of my story, but never talked about it with either one of my parents. My father's death had rendered the silence between us permanent, but my mother was still very much alive. Although we maintained reasonable, even affectionate, contact with each other, tacit disapproval from my mother had become an ingrained part of my life. Each time I felt it, I told myself it didn't matter anymore. But it did. After three decades of an imposed silence that had gone on for so long it had almost acquired a physical presence, my mother and I finally had an all-out, drop-the-gloves, let-it-all-fly, no-holds-barred argument.

Our clash began when I dared to criticize my mother's response to a situation in one of my sibling's lives. My mother has never taken well to criticism, so I knew she would be stewing about my comments. When my phone rang mid-morning a few days later, I sensed that it was my mother on the other end. I knew we would have a difficult conversation, so I braced myself, told myself to remain calm. But I failed almost immediately, and our phone call soon escalated into an avalanche of pent-up accusations about issues ranging from my father's death all the way back to my teenage pregnancy. I had never before put my feelings into words that my mother could hear. Predictably, the call ended badly. She hung up on me, and I flung the telephone across my living room floor.

Our argument was not about blame. No mother needs to have more blame heaped on her than our society is already only too willing to bestow. Our argument was about what we needed from each other. My mother needed reassurance from me that she had been a good mother. As for me, I was surprised to discover that, even thirty years later, I needed my mother to understand and acknowledge what the long-term effects of putting my first child up for adoption had been for me.

My mother wouldn't answer her phone the day after our argument or the day after that, so I soon stopped calling. About a week later, I received a letter from her. A few weeks after that, I received another one. Her letters attempted to correct what she viewed as inaccurate memories I have of the events surrounding my first pregnancy.

In response, I sent my mother a book, Anne Petrie's *Gone to an Aunt's*, the only book I've ever read about homes for unwed mothers in Canada. I know my mother didn't read it because the book came back to me almost immediately. In my mind's eye, I could picture her unwrapping the parcel, reading the title, wrapping it right back up again, and firing it into the mail as fast as she could.

As for her letters, I didn't respond to my mother's first letter, but I decided to answer the second one. I tried to explain once again, in what I hoped was a more rational approach than I had taken on the phone, my version of what had happened back in 1968 and why. I also asked her not to write me any more letters. They made me sad because I realized that she was probably never going to hear what I had to say, no matter how I said it.

I didn't think my mother was ever going to hear me because she knew now that my memories of being her daughter did not fit in with her vision of herself as a mother. It's not her fault really. She was only seventeen when her own mother died suddenly, an event I don't believe she ever completely recovered from. And she was not much more than a girl herself when she had me two weeks before her twentieth birthday. She became the mother of five children during the June Cleaver and Betty Anderson era, those television versions of motherhood that refused to acknowledge women as anything but mothers, that denied them their multiple talents and unrealized potential, that erased them as thinking beings capable of contributing to life beyond that stupid, imaginary white picket fence that may as well have been constructed out of barbed wire.

Completely indoctrinated into their social climate, many women who became mothers in that suffocating era totally lost touch with who they were or could have been. Any visions they may have had of themselves that fell outside society's version of how good wives and mothers should behave soon dissipated as the realities of their domestic lives took over. As they grew older, women like my mother needed reassurance that they had performed their prescribed roles successfully and appropriately. They needed this reassurance so that they would never have to see how the rigidity of their society's values and beliefs had constricted their lives.

Indeed, I don't think women like my mother could have handled the realization that the trajectory of their lives had been shaped by anything other than their own freely made choices. In fact, I think that if they suddenly did have insight into how their culture had trapped them, the realization of what they had lost would be too much. To avoid this realization, women like my mother worked hard to hang on to the very structures that contained them. The day of our big argument, my mother was furious with me because I was asking her to think about things she had avoided thinking about all her life.

My mother and I didn't speak to each other for almost a year. Finally, I couldn't stand the situation any longer. I dialled her number and she answered her phone. I invited her to have lunch with me. She asked where we would eat, and I said it was her choice. She said she would think about it. She called me back the next day and accepted my invitation with a condition: she would have lunch with me, but I couldn't buy it for her. She would make lunch for us at her condo. A few days later, I drove from Edmonton to Calgary for our date. We were overly cautious and polite with each other at first. Then we relaxed a little, talked about my children, my various nieces and nephews. It felt good to be with my mother again after our long separation. I helped her serve our lunch. We ate and laughed together.

It was inevitable that our conversation would venture into the dangerous territory that had triggered our estrangement. We talked about our argument and started arguing again. I tried to leave and she blocked the door. Then I blurted out a question I suddenly realized I had needed to ask her for decades: "How could you ever have let me give up a child?" She looked at me blankly. After a long pause, she said, "There's something I should tell you, but . . ." I jumped in eagerly. Too eagerly. "What is it, Mom? Tell me. Tell me." Her jaw tightened and she shook her head: "No. It's nothing." I begged her to finish what she had started to say. She shook her head again. Several long minutes passed.

Then, in the calm, almost detached voice I had come to know well over the years, she said that the adoption had worked out well for everyone, that I had been fine afterwards. She said that I had gone on with my life just as I should have, that there had been no other choice. She told me how relieved she had been that I hadn't ruined my life after all. Then she hugged me and said that she was glad I finally understood what had really happened back then. Then I left. The next week we talked as if nothing had happened at all. I resigned myself to the realization that my unanswered questions would remain that way.

My mother and I have never had, will never have, an easy relationship, but at least we have a relationship. I learned a few lessons during the year of our argument. I learned that being estranged from my mother was hard, that being mad at my mother was a horrible feeling, that I needed my mother in my life. Another thing I learned is that I can't make my mother accept my version of my adoption experience any more than she can make me accept hers.

CHAPTER TWELVE

A Long Labour

I HAVE ALWAYS BEEN A READER. From the first time I walked into the little library not far from the house with the broken two to this very day, reading has been a constant love in my life. I get lost for hours in bookstores. I can't stand in a grocery store lineup without flipping through a magazine. I don't just look at the pictures. Sometimes the person behind me in line has to tap me on the shoulder because I've become absorbed in an article.

When I was a busy mother of young children, the grocery store was where I usually bought my reading material, but soon the conventional array of popular novels beside the cash register no longer appealed to me. Even if the title was a new one, I felt as if I already knew the story that waited inside its covers.

Once my children were all in school, I decided I would start going to a library again. On my first visit, I came out with an armload of books, books by Margaret Laurence, Margaret Atwood, and Alice Munro, none of whom I had encountered in my high school reading. I discovered that they all wrote about people and places I recognized. I lost myself in their fiction for a few years. Throughout the eighties and early nineties, my choice of reading material shifted often. When I wearied of fiction, I turned to non-fiction and began to read biographies, especially about women: Mary Queen of Scots, Eleanor Roosevelt, Golda Meir.

One Christmas morning, I unwrapped a small gift and Carol Shields's *The Stone Diaries* fell into my hands, given to me by a thoughtful friend who shares my love of reading. Although I devoured the book from beginning to end, I felt uneasy about it, perhaps because I didn't want to get to the end of a life, as Shields's protagonist Daisy Flett had, only to find myself living in a rest home surrounded by old people, not knowing whether I'm dreaming or dead. I was reminded of my grandmother, who refused to join in the social groups at her nursing home because they were filled with little old ladies. But I kept reading, and soon had read many more works by Shields. My bedside table usually has a pile of books on it, three or five or even seven. I'm often reading several of them at the same time.

As I read, I get ideas. Over the years, some ideas have been so insistent that they jump into my head and just won't leave me alone until I write them down somewhere. Sometimes they stay in my head for several days, until I can't think of anything else and reach in exasperation for the closest notebook I can lay my hands on. Once I write out whatever is in my head, my brain relaxes and the idea always leaves me in peace for a while, maybe forever. Sometimes it returns a few months later, expanded or in an entirely different form. Then I have to find where I wrote it down in the first place so I can add the new version and get it out of my head once again. I have a pile of notebooks of various shapes and sizes in a corner of my home office. These days, when I'm writing and can't think of anything to say, I pick one of them up and start flipping through my old words.

Some time after my sessions with the psychologist who fired me as a patient, I started writing what I thought was fiction: uneven, somewhat whiny stories featuring characters that all ended up looking like mirror images of me. I threw most of them out. But I kept a few: a piece about my mother's ability to make gravy and a short story about an unwed mother who has one chance to hold her baby before she leaves the hospital without him. Revised versions of both those stories appear in this book.

My work in the film industry started me writing in a different genre. An odd workplace, a film set has an aura of glamour from the outside that dissipated for me almost as soon as I stepped inside its sphere. Filled with individuals trying to stand out in an environment that is all about being highly visible, working as part of a film crew is at once fascinating and tedious. I spent hours standing around waiting for a few minutes of intense activity that led immediately to yet another long wait. In need of something to do to fill that time, I started creating weird little dramas, all featuring female protagonists conflicted about their situation as mothers or non-mothers.

I submitted some of my creations to various publications; I always received ever-so-polite rejection letters in return. My dramas were better than my poems or my short stories. I knew this because I received nicer rejection letters in response to them and even the occasional letter of interest. I wrote a short film script about a single mother trying to understand her relationships with both her deceased father and her very much alive fifteen-year-old son. To my surprise, it won a drama prize from the National Screen Institute. My prize allowed me the opportunity to refine my good script into a better story from which I created a bad short film that has a few wonderful moments in it.

Motivated by that modest success, I continued writing. I decided to work on a feature-length screenplay and created a story about a middle-aged woman who had abandoned her son and wanted back into his life ten years later. I was elated when my script attracted the interest of a Los Angeles production company.

I obediently rewrote the story according to their directions. The producers were concerned that audiences would reject my female protagonist because she was a mother who left her child in the care of his father to pursue a life of her own. Mainstream society does not look kindly on mothers who don't behave as mothers are supposed to, and the kind of movies mainstream producers make have to be what mainstream society wants to see. To broaden my story's appeal, the production company asked me to make the mother more at fault in her situation; they asked me to make her child older when she abandoned him; they asked me to make her son much more resistant to his returning mother's advances; they asked me to punish her more than I had in the original story.

After reading the finished product they had orchestrated, the production company praised me for revising the story so well. Then they declined to take my finished script into production. It fell into what is known in the industry as "development hell," and I fell into a state of, if not despair, then certainly mild dejection.

It seemed to be a pattern in my life: for one reason or another, I couldn't commit to any one career for longer than about seven years. Some people run into a so-called seven-year itch in their personal relationships with their life partners; I find myself susceptible to a seven-year itch in my relationship with my work. After throwing myself into an endeavour with enthusiasm and energy, about seven years later, something always goes wrong or seems to be missing.

This time, Alberta politics had a sudden, direct impact on my life. When Ralph Klein, then premier of Alberta, dealt an almost fatal blow to my province's motion picture industry during the deficit onslaught he unleashed in the mid-nineties, my work as a stills photographer dried up almost immediately. Unwilling to leave my family to chase after film work in other parts of the country, I knew I had to make yet another change.

I had never lost the desire to go to university. I don't know why, but the lure of campus life, the mystique of academia, the aura of credibility, and the calm sureness of intellectual prowess that I thought I saw surrounding those in that world had magnetic powers for me. Had I gone that route back when my uncle offered to pay my university tuition, my life would surely have been different. Now in my forties, I didn't want a different life. I just wanted to go to university.

I had tried once before. Back in the Maritimes after the birth of my eldest daughter, I started working toward an undergraduate degree in psychology. When she was not quite a year old, I strapped my baby into the backpack she loved to ride in, adjusted it squarely on my shoulders, and walked up the hill to the University of New

Brunswick campus where I registered as a B.A. student and signed my daughter up for the part-time daycare centre run by UNB's child psychology students. We both thrived. She charmed the people at her daycare, and I took to my schoolwork immediately, enjoyed my classes, studied hard, and did well.

When we moved to Edmonton the following summer, I planned to continue working on my degree by registering for part-time studies once we got settled in our new city and our second child had safely arrived. When that second child turned out to be twins, I put my university plans on hold for a few years. As it turned out, they stayed on hold for much longer than I anticipated.

So, in the mid-nineties, with my notions of becoming a successful screenwriter stalled and my career as a stills photographer in the Alberta film industry suddenly at a standstill, I decided it was time for me to turn my attention back to my university goals. Instead of picking up where I left off—I had wanted to become a child psychologist—I had a new plan. I would pursue a degree in film studies with a secondary focus on writing. Then I would go back to that Los Angeles production company with a perfected script and show them what they passed up. But, as has happened often in my life, what I planned to do was not what I did.

I started out slowly. The first year I went part-time, taking two evening classes. They went well, so the next year I became a full-time student at the University of Alberta. Day classes were much different than evening classes. In the evenings, there were always some students my age or even older. Not so in the daytime. Sometimes, as a so-called mature student sitting in a room filled with classmates who were almost all younger than any of my children, I imagined what I would have been like as a university student when I was still a teenager.

I likely would have been much like the students that surrounded me now. I likely would have thought it was a great time to be young. I would have been a girl of my era, a packet of birth control pills tucked in my purse, bell-bottom blue jeans fraying at the edges, tie-dyed T-shirts layered over with beads and perhaps a fur vest in the style of Janis Joplin, my long straight hair parted in the middle swaying in the breeze and falling over my face as I read Betty Friedan and Germaine Greer while listening to Helen Reddy sing her female anthem, "I am woman. Hear me roar."

I have no doubt that I would have found a group of like-minded young women who wanted to reject the tedious lives of their mothers. Those lives would not be for strong, liberated young women like us. Although we would have been at university to achieve our educational goals, we would have met young men, suitors who would have been all for our independence, enticed by our intoxicating vitality, our ambition, our sexiness, especially our sexiness. They would have wanted us. Some would have asked us to marry them.

Some of us would have said yes, envisioning marriages nothing like our parents had. We would have known that our men weren't charming princes, just as we were no slumbering princesses. We would have been certain that we would be equal partners who made decisions together, built lives together, had families together. We could have it all, we would have thought. What we wouldn't have known was that many of those young men wanted their sexy, fascinating girlfriends to become wives who would stay sexy and fascinating at the same time as they did everything for them that their mothers had done.

But I wasn't a teenager at university in the seventies. It was almost the end of the twentieth century, and I was a middle-aged woman determined to get everything I could out of my delayed academic experience. In my second full-time year, I registered for an English course in something called literary theory, having absolutely no idea what it was going to be about. I liked the sound of it and it fit into my schedule. It turned out to be a broad survey that ran the gamut of past and current literary thinking: from formalism to structuralism to deconstruction to gender theory to sexuality to feminism.

From day one, I was awash in words and thoughts. Confused and destabilized, appalled and mesmerized, I began to identify with feminists. I suddenly found myself acutely aware of the dilemmas of the various women's movements, especially the second wave I had hardly noticed as I lived through it. Still out of sync with my times, I was not yet completely wise to the fact that my moment of realization was happening in the midst of the more current third wave, itself about to tumble into post-feminism or wherever it is we are now.

Calmly watching as her students waded through this torrent of material, my professor was engaging, informed, dynamic, and highly adept at conveying optimistic comfort while simultaneously filling her students' minds with new knowledge that challenged almost any conventional belief system. She had my complete attention.

At the end of that course, I was hooked and changed my direction. Instead of film studies, I decided to major in English. I went to see that captivating professor and asked if she thought I was too old to consider going to graduate school. Absolutely not was her answer. A year later, I had the degree I had wanted for so long, but I didn't want to stop there. I wanted to go all the way. I applied for postgraduate studies.

The next fall, on a sunny September morning, I looked in the mirror and saw an old grad student. My children had successfully completed their university programs and were out building their own lives. I was still a student, ready to embark on a master's program in which I planned to focus on contemporary Canadian women writers. Very soon, I realized that life in graduate studies was a maze of contrasts: stimulating and daunting, exciting and demoralizing, confidence-building and anxiety-producing. I diligently went to all my seminars, participated in their discussions, and spent hours in the library. I read and studied every moment that I could, wrote what seemed like a hundred essays, and soon discovered that my graduate student life caused havoc in my personal life.

With every theory I read, I became angrier. With every new insight into the injustices of the past, I became more strident. With every essay I produced, I became more obsessed with making sure that everyone around me knew that we had all been indoctrinated to accept flawed ideals in our lives. The more I read, the more I could not shed the notion that many people are merely puppets to the status quo. How had I not seen this for so long?

I argued with my husband and my friends; I alienated my sisters and caused my nieces and nephews to look at me with not a little fear; I lectured anyone who would listen about the evils built into the very substance of our society. I struggled to get through a maze of reading and research that stimulated me in my work but stymied me in my personal life. Not surprisingly, I was alone a lot and more than a little lonely.

During this time, it seemed to me that the only people in my immediate sphere who didn't think that going back to university had permanently ruined me were my children. Despite what many of my friends and family thought of as my weird behaviour, my three young adults were calm, perhaps somewhat amused by it all. They seemed even proud of what I was doing and were always steadfast in their support for me. Whenever I asked them how they felt about my university studies, they replied as a unit: go Mom go. It's not that I was asking permission. I simply wanted their support, and they gave it unconditionally.

I completed the requirements for my master's degree in one year and went directly into a Ph.D. program, still in the English department, still at the University of Alberta. That summer, I prepared myself for a dramatically increased workload. In addition to all the new coursework I had to complete, I was also assigned teaching duties as sole instructor for a freshman English course.

I met my first students on a beautiful September day. Our initial session together was just a preliminary meeting where I went over the syllabus for the year. I spent the following weekend nervously preparing for my first real day as a university teacher. That day was Tuesday, September 11, 2001.

Early that morning, after my husband left for work, I sat down to put the finishing touches on my lecture notes. A few minutes later, my husband rushed back into the house and turned on the television. He and I watched in shock as the second plane hit the World Trade Center in New York, were still watching when the towers fell not long afterwards. I went to campus in a numbed state. Prior to my eleven o'clock class, I walked up and down the halls of the department looking for a professor to talk to, someone I could ask how to make Shakespeare's sonnets relevant on a day like this. I finally found one. His advice was curt. "You can't," he said. "Don't even try."

In spite of that unnerving start to my teaching career, I discovered that I very much enjoyed my experience at the front of a classroom. My initial nervousness died down quickly. I had feared that I wouldn't be of much use to my students, but found instead that I was indeed able to help them as they progressed through the dizzying whirl of first-year university. I enjoyed seeking out stories, poems, and novels to include in our studies. I enjoyed planning our class time and creating writing assignments. I did not enjoy marking, but I have yet to meet an English professor who does. Most of all, I enjoyed showing my students how to use language effectively, how language conveys meaning, how to believe in their abilities to interpret a difficult text. I was, however, and still am, dismayed at the poor level of the writing and grammar skills they brought with them from high school. From what I could see, the teaching of high school English had deteriorated badly since my days in the first row of Mr. Arnason's class.

Over the next few years, along with my teaching duties, I had my own work to deal with. I had looming written and oral exams to pass. I had to find a dissertation project, then write and ultimately defend it. I had time for little else. While I developed a few close relationships among my grad student colleagues, as someone who seemed decidedly ancient to most of them, I wasn't comfortable joining in their evening bar gatherings or even attending social events put on by the English department. Mostly, I did my teaching work, went to the library, and disappeared to my home office to study, write, and live my non-university life.

My husband, to his credit, never asked me to abandon my strange obsession with university, and always supported me by providing both the physical and emotional space I needed to do my work, even when I stopped referring to him as my husband. For a while, I decided to use the more intellectually acceptable term *partner* instead. I had adopted the academic argument that the stereotype accompanying the words *wife* and *husband* carried far too much negative baggage. After a while, he became my husband again because every time I used the word *partner* he thought I was referring to someone else, someone I must have started a business with, a venture I must have neglected to tell him about.

Like many grad students, I didn't sleep well during this period of my life. The circles under my eyes darkened. Instead of lying awake in bed, I often wrapped my housecoat around me and went into my office, now filled with overloaded shelves, boxes of books, and stacked binders of finished writing sitting beside piles of unfinished papers topped with scattered pages of handwritten notes. In the middle of the night, I would find my chair amid all this clutter and dive into my computer.

During this time, I discovered something about myself: I like computers. I had been curious about computers as soon as they came into our lives. As I grew more adept at using them, I discovered that I liked them a lot. I should have known that about myself already. After all, I like using most electronic devices. Whether it's a camera or a cellphone or a computer, as soon as I get one I read all the instructions because, whatever the device, I have a strong desire to become more than competent using it.

The first computer I worked on was nothing more than a word processor, a huge machine with a dark black screen and glowing lime-green letters. As everyone knows, those clunky first computers soon evolved into life-changing machines. When the Internet grew into a force not to be ignored, my world changed. Web-surfing became my one of my favourite indoor sports.

After I got my first home computer and I could browse the Internet in private, it didn't take long for me to do a search using *adoption* as my keyword. Through that search, I discovered something I had never imagined: a large online community of people affected by adoption. I also discovered a host of post-adoption registries, organizations that I might never have known about without computers.

I had known that some adoption organizations existed. I had once joined an Alberta group that welcomed both birth parents and adoptees. I read about it in a small local magazine, sent in a membership application, and soon received a welcoming letter that invited me to attend their next meeting. I thought about it, but I didn't go. Ever. I noted the date each time a meeting approached, intended to go, but at the last minute always decided that I had something else more important to do. The next day, I would rail at myself for such cowardice. When it came time to renew, I let my membership lapse and turned my attention to other things.

In the world of graduate studies, everyone has a particular focus, a specific concentration, a niche of scholarly expertise. "What is your area?" is an often-heard phrase in university corridors, coming from professors, administrators, and—perhaps most often—our grad student colleagues. I strongly resisted this constant academic pressure to choose one particular specialty. Whenever anyone asked me what my area was, I cringed inside. I don't think I ever gave the same answer twice. I wanted to try out different answers to see how they sounded out loud. Once in the air, each statement felt like I was climbing back into a box. I'd spent most of my adult life knocking down the boxes that contained me. Why did I have to build myself a new box?

I wanted to study contemporary Canadian women writers, which was fine, but as a dissertation topic it was a bust. At first, I thought I wanted to focus on novels. Then I read Michael Ondaatje and Thomas King and wondered why I should limit my work only to women authors. I don't remember what novel I was reading when I came up with the idea of investigating writers of the baby boom generation. I was curious about what kind of stories baby boom writers created about the society they had had such an impact on. I would call it "Boomerlit." I was excited by that prospect. Unfortunately, no one else was.

I had to find a supervisor for my dissertation project, so I took my idea to some of the professors in my department. I sat in their offices explaining what I wanted to do. They asked me questions I hadn't considered. Was it going to be about writers who wrote about the baby boom period, or would it be writers who were born as part of the baby boom? Didn't baby boom writers write about a lot of topics? How was I going to narrow it down? One professor burst out laughing when I told him my tentative title was "Boomerlit." I retreated from his office as fast as I could.

I began to realize that not everyone liked the baby boom generation. In fact, while boomer-bashing hadn't yet escalated to the journalistic national sport it seems to be now, many people were downright insulting about baby boomers, about our apparent greediness, about how we abandoned our ideals. When I didn't find any support in my department for a Boomerlit dissertation, I was sad, but returned to my pile of Canadian novels to search for a new idea, one that was focused, more specific.

Contemporary Canadian writing is rich in content, widely diverse in origin: Nino Ricci, Hiromi Goto, Eden Robinson, Kerri Sakamoto, Rohinton Mistry. The list is long and tantalizing, the backgrounds of so many of these writers much different from mine, which was probably why I was drawn to their writing. I was just a prairie girl from a predominantly white Anglo-Saxon neighbourhood in South Winnipeg. I started to feel small. My life was ordinary, I thought. My experience range is bland, I thought.

And that's when I stopped myself. That's when I realized that graduate work not only expands thinking processes, but can also undermine them. I scolded myself: *Stop wallowing. You have lived widely within the framework of who you are: a middle-aged, middle-class, white, heterosexual woman.* And there was my answer. I went back to writers who were like me. I went back to writers who had lived or were living lives similar to mine. I went into their work to examine the imagined stories that come out of lived experiences like ours.

I started working to define a project. However, ever-chafing at being confined, I still wanted to find ways for me to reach out of my specialty box. While reading through Jane Urquhart's novels, I came upon what I thought was a unique solution. Urquhart weaves many references and allusions to other writers and visual artists into her stories, giving them strong intertextual connections. I found this an appealing feature. I would ground my thesis in her work and use intertextuality as my method of investigation. I could stand in the present, in my known world, and use my intertextual approach to visit other countries and romp through time. Ecstatic, I wrote out my idea and went knocking on professor doors again.

This time, I did find a supervisor who was interested, and the graduate committee accepted my thesis proposal. I passed my candidacy exams and started to write my dissertation. I was exhilarated and filled with enthusiasm. Using Urquhart's portrayal of Robert Browning in *The Whirlpool*, I jumped into his Victorian works. Using Urquhart's allusions to Percy Bysshe Shelley, I took a jump back to the age of the Romantics. I was having fun. It seemed too good to be true, to have fun while writing a dissertation.

On an intertextual high, I took many imaginative voyages across the Atlantic Ocean. I also made one literal journey, a research trip to put myself at the base of Walter Allward's Vimy Ridge monument, on the narrow streets of Venice searching for Tintoretto's Scuola San Rocco, inside the walls of the National Gallery in London seeking various artistic versions of St. George, the dragon, and the ever-present damsel in distress. My excitement stayed with me. If this strategy worked, I thought with more than a little glee, after I finished this project, I could go to Africa with Margaret Laurence, back to London with Carol Shields, down to New York with Elizabeth Smart.

A year later, I was no longer excited. I was exhausted and not a little dizzy. I felt that my writing had become robotic. I wanted my thesis project to be fascinating and exotic. It wasn't. My supervisor seemed to think it was coming along nicely. I thought it was too unwieldy and too predictable at the same time. I thought it was leading nowhere. I thought I had created a dissertation nightmare, a journey without a destination, a process instead of an argument. Determined to finish anyway, I made myself sit down and write. I had produced over a hundred pages. I was more than halfway there. Just keep writing, I told myself.

At this point, in the middle of learning and teaching, of spending sleepless nights at my computer, of writing a dissertation I no longer liked but hoped to finish, things took an unexpected turn. The son I surrendered to the closed adoption system in 1968 came back into my life.

CHAPTER THIRTEEN

Birthmother

I SUPPOSE IT WAS INEVITABLE that I would eventually investigate the history of adoption. My academic studies taught me how to conduct research into almost any topic, whether I was on campus prowling through the stacks of the humanities library or at home sitting in my pyjamas in front of my computer. Whenever an item about adoption caught my eye, I always looked it over, no matter what else I was working on.

The first adoption regulations in Canada came into force during the 1920s. Prior to then, most adoptions were privately arranged. Birth families and adoptive families often knew each other, were perhaps even branches of the same family, sometimes close neighbours. As the twentieth century progressed, concern grew about continued contact between the birth family and the adoptive family. Prevailing social tendency was to give the adopting family priority as the ideal environment for the child. Birth families were increasingly viewed as lacking competence. If they happened to be poor, it was worse for them: they were even more likely to be considered unfit.

After the violence of World War II, western society wanted a fresh start, order after the chaos of conflict. Adopting families were needed. They had social approval and moral support. As adoption records grew more formalized, adopting families also had legal support. Authorities began to seal adoption records permanently to protect and privilege those they viewed as "respectable" families. In this climate, the closed adoption system came to be the most dominant form of adoption for more than two decades. This system was ruled by secrecy and rooted in shaming the birth mother and her family. It largely dismissed the notion that any desirable bond existed between a biological mother and the child she put up for adoption.

During the 1970s, the closed adoption system began to shut down as the social stigma of an unmarried woman having a child gradually started to lose its power. By the 1980s, movements toward opening sealed adoption records had begun, but only on behalf of the adoptee, not the relinquishing parents.

In January of 1995, making use of advice I found while browsing the Internet, I wrote to Manitoba Family Services, inquiring about the son I gave up for adoption in 1968. I asked for whatever information they could give me about him and said that I would be receptive to having contact with him should he ever decide to look for me.

A few weeks later, I received a brief letter from the Manitoba Post-Adoption Registry. The letter informed me that provincial legislation prohibited them from searching for my son at my request, even though I had not requested this action. Included with the letter was a pamphlet outlining the Registry's services and fees. I read through it and talked to my husband. Although he encouraged me to put my name on the registry, he was also concerned that I would get my hopes up and surely be disappointed.

I didn't tell him that my hopes were already up. I was sure that placing my name on this registry would result in contact with my son. I reasoned that he would be a smart person, that if he wanted to find me, the first place he would go would be the post-adoption registry associated with the organization that had originally placed him.

I sent off the completed registration form along with a cheque. Six weeks after that, I received another letter from Manitoba Family Services acknowledging receipt of my registration form. The letter said that my son had not filed a corresponding inquiry and reminded me again that Manitoba law allowed them to search for birth parents on behalf of an adult adoptee but did not allow them to search for an adopted child on behalf of a birth parent. The letter ended by saying that it would take them several months to find the non-identifying information I had requested about my son.

One year and nine months later, I received a response to my information request signed by the same person who had responded to my first two letters. He apologized for the lengthy delay and informed me that they had had no contact with my son since I signed the final adoption papers. Along with the letter, he included a sheet containing virtually the same non-identifying information I had been given just after my son's adoption back in 1968 with a few extra sentences added about what a good baby he had been at age four months. I read through this meagre, decades-old commentary over and over again, looking at and between the words for anything concrete I could grab onto, anything to help me ascertain that he was alive and well.

The letter from Manitoba Family Services also informed me—in capital letters no less—that they were enclosing a copy of the adoption consent form I had signed in 1968, eleven days after my son's birth. This took me aback a little, because, over the years, I had erased that moment from my mind. But I recognized the document immediately. The layout of the page was familiar, with the sturdy bison of the Manitoba provincial crest featured at the top and my personal information inserted in the required blank spaces. In bold, blurry letters, it identifies me as the mother of the named "out of wedlock" child, as a student (which I wasn't at that time), and as giving my authorization for the adoption "of my own free will and accord."

Ever since the day I signed that paper, I had suppressed the moment so deeply that I hadn't been able to call it up in my memory at all. But, as I sat looking at the signature my eighteen-year-old hand had provided, the scene flooded back to me. I remembered that I hadn't said much. I remembered how I could hardly move, much less speak; how I couldn't read through most of the words because my brain refused to process them; how I felt when I came to condition number eight: "I will not . . . at any time . . . molest, disturb . . . or interfere with . . . the upbringing of [my] child." I remembered how the word *molest* had stabbed at me back then. *They thought I was going to molest my baby?* Although my signature looks steady, I remembered how the inside muscles of my arm trembled as my hand scrawled out my name. I remembered that I barely responded to their parting comments.

I can't remember myself actually leaving that appointment, so I have to imagine it. I see my eighteen-year-old self straightening my back as I rise from a stiff-backed chair to walk out of that room, perhaps down a long hallway, departing silently but with very good posture, as if I had been kicked in the stomach and the butt at the same time.

More than two-and-a-half decades later, I sat in my comfortable home and read through all the papers I received from Manitoba Family Services several times. Suddenly, I felt small again. I felt the edict of silence working on me again. I started to feel shame again. And I realized that, even as the closed adoption system had largely crumbled, the attitudes that shaped it were still active in the adoption world. The adoptee's family must be protected at all costs, and I was one of those costs. Women like me who had surrendered our "out of wedlock" children to adoption must be kept as uninformed and docile as possible. One way of doing that was to intimidate inquisitive birthmothers by sending them hard copies of old documents bearing their youthful signatures.

After a few weeks of staring at that adoption consent form, I put it and the letters in a file in my desk and went back to the business of living my life. The rest of the nineties played out. The tension-filled buildup to Y2K came and went. My family and I had a wonderful New Year as the year 2000 rolled in without catastrophic computer-related incidents. Nothing fell out of the sky and the world continued to function as usual. That winter and spring, we drank the bottled water I had stored in our basement as our emergency supply for when the world stopped turning.

By the time the new millennium rolled in, I had reconciled myself to the idea that I would probably never know anything more about my lost child. After all, by this time, he was a fully grown man in his thirties, likely far past the age when he may have been pulled by urges to seek out an anonymous woman long gone from his life.

Around then, I rediscovered someone intimately involved in the creation of my son's life. In what now seems like an auspicious coincidence, I happened to reconnect briefly with my baby's father. Although we had not seen or been in touch with each other for over thirty years, I had always known where he was. Not that I was stalking him or anything like that, but every time I visited the city he had moved to, I checked the telephone book to see if he was still listed. In the back of my mind, I nurtured a small hope that if I could ever talk to our son, I would want to be able to tell him who and where his father was.

Again, the Internet offered assistance. When our former high school held a reunion, it was advertised on a website with a message board. One of my sisters posted a message on it. My former boyfriend saw and sent her a message asking where I was. She forwarded it to me, and I answered him right away. His reply came quickly. He said that he would soon be in Edmonton on a business trip and wondered if we could have dinner together. Without hesitation, I said yes. I asked my husband to join us, but he graciously said I should go on my own. So I did.

We had a terrific reunion that evening, reminiscing about our time together, sharing our life experiences, and telling each other stories about our families—both the ones we came from and the ones we had created in the ensuing years. I soon remembered what good friends we had been, how much we had enjoyed each other's company. As the evening progressed and we grew more comfortable talking with each other, I ventured into a more serious topic.

I told him about placing my name on the post-adoption registry so that our son could find me if he ever decided to look. We talked briefly about launching a search for him together, but came to the conclusion that even now it was not our prerogative to disrupt his life. Perhaps a little fear about what we might find also held us back. A question I had never allowed myself to consider for very long always lurked in the back of my mind: How would I feel if I discovered that my child had had a terrible life? As we parted that evening, I promised my newly found old friend that if our son ever did contact me, I would let him know.

Several years passed. Then, on a cold October day in 2004, I came home from my morning teaching duties intending to spend the afternoon working on my dissertation. Before settling into my writing chair, I flipped through the newspaper and absentmindedly turned on my answering machine. A quiet female voice filled my kitchen: "Call this number for an important personal message." At first I thought it was merely another telemarketer and I moved to erase it. Just before I hit that button, I glanced at the call display: the phone number had a Manitoba area code. Nah, it couldn't be, I thought, but I dialled the number anyway. A woman with one of the most soothing voices I've ever heard took my call. Very calmly, as if asking me if I'd forgotten to pick up last week's dry cleaning, she said that the son I had given up for adoption so many years ago wanted to make contact with me.

In my mind, that moment has become one of those slow-motion, real-life montages often associated with cinematic chase scenes, car crashes, or other near-death experiences (without the near-death part). Instead of a hurricane of emotions, I felt an overwhelming calm. The woman with the soothing voice asked how I would like to handle the situation. I replied that I would prefer to exchange letters first because I'm better with written words than spoken ones in awkward situations. As it turned out, my son felt exactly the same way. Through the social worker, we exchanged names and addresses.

I wrote him a letter that afternoon: it is the only finished piece of writing I have ever produced that I did not revise several times. That letter poured out of me intact as if I had been working on it for years, and in a sense I had. I told him what had happened back in 1968 and why. This was especially important to me, because I had always wanted him to know that he was the result of a loving relationship, not an act of violence or a fleeting encounter. I told him what had happened in my life (the cheerfully abridged version) since that time and what my life was like now. I told him that every year his birthday was a day of yearning for me. I told him I had one picture of him, taken when he was about three days old, that I have kept in my night table drawer since the day I got it.

In a coincidence we both like, my son and I received each other's letters on exactly the same day. I was elated when I read the first sentence in his letter: "The first thing I want to tell you is that

I'm doing great." I tried not to feel hurt by his next comment: "Thank you for making the right decision to hand me over for adoption." That line felt coached, as if an adoption agency had written it. Adoption wasn't a "decision" for me. Making a decision implies that more than one choice is available. My society, my community, my doctors, the hospital staff, the social workers, and my family all had made certain that I had no other choices.

But a smile came to my face as I read through the rest of his letter. I could see he wanted to make a good impression on me, because it looked almost like a resumé. I felt much pride as I read through his credits as a university graduate and learned about his successful career. I was relieved to hear that his parents had always loved and cared for him well. He included pictures of himself as a child. They blurred as I pored over each one of them.

Just as I had done in my letter to him, my son had provided me with his email address. After I had absorbed the letter and his pictures several times over, I went to my computer to put his address in my directory. A message instantly popped up from him.

For the next few weeks, we kept our email inboxes buzzing as we exchanged words and pictures in a steady stream. In his wedding photographs, I was stunned to see a younger version of my father's face staring out at me. I sent him a picture of my father so he could see the resemblance for himself. Everyone who saw their two faces side by side was struck by how much they look like each other. My brother said that had he ever passed my son on the street, he would have walked up and introduced himself.

Each day I raced home to my computer looking for the latest message. Our reunion took over my life. I could think about little else for months. I managed to keep up with my teaching duties, but my dissertation lay untouched in its pile, abandoned. Occasionally, I looked at it questioningly. What was it about again?

When he was ready, my son decided that it was time for us to meet in person. I arranged flights as soon as possible. My husband and I flew to Winnipeg. I think I checked my reflection in the mirror at least a hundred times as we waited for a knock on our hotel room door. My husband told me to relax. I gave him my best "you've got to be kidding" look. He responded by saying that I looked fine. I checked the mirror again.

The knock finally came. I raced to the door, paused for a deep breath, and flung it open. And there he was: tall, smiling, holding his wife's hand. I don't remember the words, just the big long hug. As the four of us had dinner together that night, talk was constant with no strained silences.

The next morning, I met his parents. His mother brought me a rose, and we both cried as we greeted each other. I struggled to keep my composure when she said that I had given them the most wonderful gift possible. I felt strangely wounded by that comment, as if I had wrapped my baby up with a big blue ribbon and willingly sent him off as a present to strangers. But I hid my wound because I didn't want to spoil the moment. I also found myself reverting back in time. Instead of the mature woman I was, I felt as if I were that scared eighteen-year-old girl again. She was definitely with me that morning in my son's home, as I gave and received many hugs.

My son's parents are very nice people. He adores them and

they him. Their genuine goodness is evident in how they openly welcomed me into their lives that day. Sometimes it felt as if we all were talking at the same time. We just had so much to say. For a long while, as my husband visited with my son and his wife, his parents and I shared our stories with each other. The words tumbled out. We couldn't talk fast enough. His stories. My stories. His mother told me about our son's childhood. I told them all stories about my children, the siblings he didn't yet know, but would soon.

Eventually we started talking about my extended family, more specifically about my father. In one of our earliest emails, my son had casually mentioned that his father had known my father. Winnipeg was a small city in the sixties, and my father knew a lot of people, so I wasn't that surprised. That morning, I discovered that my son's father and my father had worked in the same industry, in office buildings almost across the street from each other.

Other discoveries were more difficult for me. It was on that day that I learned about the treachery of the closed adoption process, how it fundamentally betrayed the young women who surrendered their babies to its workings. As information flowed between my son's parents and me, so did revelations about how the adoption played out on both sides. Some of the adopting agency's manipulations were relatively minor. For instance, back in 1968, perhaps intending to misdirect any future efforts I might make to find him, the social workers told me that a family living outside of Winnipeg had adopted my son. After our reunion, I found out that he has lived in Winnipeg all his life.

Other betrayals were far more serious. My son's parents told me that the social workers said they shouldn't ever worry about me coming back to make a claim on their son. I was very negative, they said, and wanted nothing to do with my child.

The social workers also told my son's parents which area of Winnipeg I lived in and described my father's personal appearance to them. My son's mother told me that she was very uncomfortable with the information they casually dropped about me: "They did everything but give us your name and phone number," she said. As soon as they could, my son's parents stopped dealing with the agency's social workers.

In a city as small as Winnipeg was back in the sixties, it didn't take long for them to piece information together. A few months after my son came into their lives, his father had been involved in enough casual conversations with people in their industry, possibly even including my father, to figure out where their baby had come from. Their identities were a secret the adoption agency fiercely shielded from me for over thirty years, but my identity was never a secret to them.

My son finally looked for me because he and his wife had applied to become adoptive parents themselves. In preparation, they attended a seminar in which they listened to young women who were planning to put their babies up for adoption. He said it was an emotional session and afterwards he decided to see if he could find me. He has told me that he didn't look for me earlier in his life because he was happy as a child and a young man. He also didn't want to upset his parents. The morning that I met them, his mother told me that they never encouraged him to look for me. They thought that he would be hurt, that I would reject him, given the negative attitude I had supposedly displayed during the adoption proceedings.

Since that weekend, I've spent a lot of time thinking about how the adoption agency represented me to my son's family. Again and again, I drive my mind back to that day in 1968 when I signed those adoption consent papers. I remember being on my own, with no one in the room present on my behalf because I was eighteen, an adult who didn't need representation.

I don't remember what was said or what the faces around the table looked like. I can't remember anyone asking me anything about how I felt; in fact, I can't remember speaking at all. I only remember doing what I had been told to do: remain silent. Yet the closed adoption system—a process that convinced me I had nothing to offer my child and silenced my voice for the rest of his life—decided that my silence was a sign of callous indifference.

In retrospect, I realize that my silence was a symptom of trauma. After being banished from my home for many months, after giving birth without the comfort of either family or nursing staff, after walking away from the only time I would ever hold my baby, I sat alone in a room with two judgmental strangers. I was an eighteen-year-old girl who had to read and understand unfamiliar words on a long legal document all by herself; whose voice was incapable of making a sound because it was reduced to a strangling sensation in her throat, a strangling sensation she would feel over and over again in the years ahead.

The language of the closed adoption system told me that I was a potential molester, that I must surrender all rights to my child, that to retain any dignity at all I had to go away, be passive, stay silent, and maintain my secret. The language of the closed adoption system told me that I had no right to know anything about my child or his family. What the language of the closed adoption system did not tell me was that the family who adopted my child could be told almost anything about me.

Despite these disturbing revelations, my reunion with my son was an astonishingly positive event. As my husband and I left Winnipeg after that first weekend visit, I knew we were at the beginning of a new story, our story. If our reunion had been the plot for a screenplay, any movie producer would surely have deemed it too rosy, too unbelievable, too blissful. But that's what I felt: pure bliss. And I embraced that feeling, even though I was well aware that bliss cannot be sustained for long. Virtually always untrustworthy, bliss overwhelms. It is an intoxicating feeling, an ecstatic epitome of joy, derived from fleeting, unstable moments. As an ending to a story, bliss is usually unsatisfying and even downright frightening. Indeed, bliss is not really an ending at all, but yet another beginning. And that's what our reunion was, a beginning. At some future point, I knew that our relationship might become strained, but for the moment, all was blissfully amazing. He was fine. I was fine. I knew who he was. He knew who I was.

After that emotional first meeting, many others followed. Several years earlier, I had told my three children about the brother they had out there somewhere. I hadn't wanted to tell them when they were younger because I was worried about what they would think of me. I didn't want them to be mad at me. I also didn't want them to take my experience as permission to try it themselves, even though I knew that they were certainly much more than teenaged versions of me. Indeed, my children are well-adjusted adults who continue to fill me with pride. But when they were no longer teenagers, I just felt they should know that somewhere out there they had another sibling. They absorbed that information with concern and kindness.

So when October of 2004 brought a sudden, surprising reunion in our family, I was very happy that my children knew about my first child's existence. When it came time to tell them that he had made contact, the moment was a positive one; they were excited and nervous, but most of all, eager to meet their brother. My son, the one whom I raised, was the first to meet his newly found sibling. They formed an immediate, easy bond. My two daughters met their new brother a few months later. They all used their mutual enjoyment of beer to get to know each other.

True to my promise, I put my son in touch with his biological father, and the same thing happened: another big family waited to know him and gather him into their midst. A few months later, six happy people—my husband and I, my son and his wife, and my former boyfriend and his wife—went on a winter holiday together, flying to a sandy resort where we spent a week getting to know each other as we drank in the sunshine (and the rum and the beer and the wine), laughing when we explained our relationship to astonished inquirers.

When summer came that year, I organized a big family lunch where my son (along with his wife and his parents) met everyone on my side of his now vastly extended family: my sisters, my brother, my brothers-in-law, my nieces and nephews, and my mother. Everyone in my family is delighted to be connected to my son's life today.

Of course, my father has missed it all. His absence is an ongoing sorrow for me. During that summer lunch, as I watched my son mingle with the relatives he had just met, I knew that my father would have loved this grandson, would have been especially pleased that his oldest grandson looks just like him, talks and sounds just like him. My son has also inherited his maternal grandfather's natural affability and keen enthusiasm for the Winnipeg Blue Bombers. I feel great grief that they never knew each other. My father was only forty-two years old when his first grandchild was born. How much the rest of his life would have been enriched by having his oldest grandson in it, I will never know, but I think it would have been a good thing for both of them.

After the initial excitement of introducing everyone settled down, my son and I began the very real task of getting to know each other. It was, and is, difficult. An intimate bond exists between mother and child at the moment of birth, a trusting connection that has been nurtured in two beings who lived together in one body for nine months. Ours had been irrevocably severed. At times, especially because we live in different cities, we seemed to move slowly in our efforts to reconnect with each other; at other times, we moved too fast.

Once we determined that we had both survived the circum-stances of his birth and gone on to live productive lives, we had to go further. We had moments when getting to know each other was a touchy process. I think he was taken aback to discover that his birthmother was, gulp, a feminist, just as I was taken aback to discover that my long-lost child was, gulp, a conservative. Having our longstanding imagined blank pictures of each other replaced by real, concrete, often charming, but inevitably flawed human beings has been a challenging experience.

In some ways, we are very similar. We both love to laugh. We both want to please our families, and we both run into difficulties when we don't. We feel our emotions deeply, but often keep them to ourselves. When we are hurt, we both tend to put on a stoic front and retreat into silence.

Moreover, we are both highly sensitive to rejection and abandonment. While perhaps expected in adoptees, this characteristic is not often associated with birthmothers. Mainstream thinking is that the adopted child is the only one abandoned, a notion that conveniently ignores just how many people and organizations had to abandon the birthmother to create the adopting situation. In getting to know both my son and myself better, I have become acutely aware of how the nailed-shut structure of the closed adoption system has left its scars on both of us.

During the first year after our reunion, my son's mother made me a gift: a photo album. In it, she created a visual record of our son's life from the day he came into their home right through all the stages of his childhood, his adolescence, and his young manhood. She wanted to explain each picture to me, so I sat beside her nodding quietly as she went through page after page. Although very grateful for her efforts, I could feel myself tightening up inside, tightening up and shutting down. I felt myself wanting to pull away from the images, a feeling I didn't understand at first.

I had made a similar photo album of my life and given it to my son. He seemed to like it. Afterwards, I hoped it hadn't caused him any of the strange discomfort I felt. I took the photo album his mother made for me home and put it in a cupboard in my office so that it's close to where I work every day. I'm happy to know that it's there, but I can't look at it. It's too painful to see what I missed all those years.

A few months afterwards, I experienced a sudden self-insight. That photo album finally allowed me to understand the numbness I've noticed in that vague place where feelings are stored in my body, the numbness that has been part of me since my son's adoption. I realized that emotional numbness is my body's method of pain management. My reaction to the photo album was similar to what happened inside me the day my father died. After the stunning, visceral impact I felt when my sister told me he was dead, a few hours later I felt only a numb calmness. I know now that when what I feel is too painful, my body won't let me feel anything at all.

Today, contemporary adoption processes have changed drastically. Significantly, the terms of reference have changed since 1968. The phrase *unwed mother* is no longer in use, replaced by the phrase *single mother*, a term that suggests more acceptance than it actually offers. As changing adoption laws allowed the opening of sealed records, contact between birth and adopting families became a more common occurrence. Further changes in the language of adoption soon resulted. Indeed, a whole new language, contested as it is, revolves around contemporary adoption processes.

The language change that affects me the most is that I am

now a *birthmother*: essentially, a mother who isn't the woman who gave birth but who is not the mother. Back in the sixties, we were "real" mothers or "natural" mothers. The switch to the term *birthmother* came about to reassure adopting mothers that they were the "real" mothers. Unsurprisingly, the language around adoption is charged with emotion. Nevertheless, when it changes, the one who comes out diminished is still usually the woman who has relinquished her child.

The first few times my son introduced me as his birthmother, I felt simultaneously pleased, distressed, and uneasy: pleased to be recognized as connected to my son, distressed because the label *birthmother* implies that any maternal feelings I had about him ended with his birth (otherwise why would I have made the "choice" to put him up for adoption), and uneasy because people have varied responses to birthmothers, even in our so-called enlightened times.

In public moments, I counsel myself to remain open and calm, but I also watch reactions carefully. Is it just my imagination, or did those eyes linger a little longer on me? Is she or he expressing genuine interest, or is it merely invasive curiosity? Was it friendliness or judgment I saw flicker across that face? Although I no longer feel any shame about what happened to me, the shaming stigmas of the sixties linger on in many ways, in many minds. I continue to teach myself how to walk away from innuendo, how to walk toward calm sincerity.

Yet, at times I still struggle with my role as birthmother. Some days, the word fills me with sadness, never letting me forget that, although he is my son, I am not his mother. Most days, however,

I am grateful. On those days, I remember the other role that was mine for over three decades, the woman with a secret, the mother with a child out there in the world somewhere, a child she can't visualize, can't name, can't hug. Today, I know where to go to hug my son.

From my son's perspective, finding his place in two big families that suddenly want him in their lives has been difficult at times. From my perspective, it's hard to know how to be an extra mother in a grown man's life. Building a relationship, maternal or otherwise, with a newly met adult child is largely uncharted territory: no Dr. Spock-like manuals exist for guidance. I've made mistakes and we've had our differences along the way. Nevertheless, although we are occasionally tentative with each other, we are, I believe, always firmly invested in making our relationship a positive one.

By the end of the twentieth century, the closed adoption system that sentenced so many young women to a grief that will never go away had become archaic. New adoption choices were available to young women, most commonly the open adoption system in which the birthmother and the adopting parents have access to each other.

A few years after our reunion, the son I relinquished to the closed adoption system made me a grandmother through the open adoption process. As soon as possible after hearing the good news, my husband and I travelled to Winnipeg to meet our infant grandson. During that weekend, with a new family treasure snuggled warm in my arms, I thought about the young woman who had given birth to him, about the years ahead for her.

Logically, her experience should be much different than mine. She knows where her child is. She actively chose her child's parents based on a list of conditions she defined. She can picture where he sleeps at night and who will tend to him when he cries. She will have information about his progress throughout his life and designated times when she can visit. She knows that her child's parents know who she is because my son and daughter-in-law have opened their door to her and watched her visit their son in their home.

I admit that I envy her active participation in finding a home for her child, that she was not marginalized and manipulated by a process steeped in punitive judgments. Nevertheless, I don't envy her situation. I wish her well and hope that, from this painful experience, she will be able to move ahead in a less judgmental world, move on to a satisfying productive life, unplagued by doubts about her decision and worries about her child. Adoption has come a long way since the sixties, but severing the bond between a biological mother and her child is always going to be a wrenching process, one that will never be without consequences.

What Is Your Name?

GRADUATE STUDENTS STUDYING in the humanities disciplines are easy to spot around university campuses and in nearby coffeehouses. Instead of spending time doing experiments in labs like their science-based colleagues, humanities students, perhaps especially those in the discipline of English, are always reading, hunched over their books as they underline key passages and make notes in the margins of their pages. When they do raise their heads from their work, each one wears a dazed expression not unlike that of a deer frozen in its tracks by the blazing headlight of an oncoming train. For six years, I felt as if I were living in the few seconds just prior to that impending collision.

After I sat down and wrote to my son for the first time, used his name for the first time, mailed a letter to his home address for the first time, I sat at my desk for several hours. Some time later I knew, for the first time, that feminism had not passed me by, that my late-in-life turn to feminist thinking hadn't come from my academic adventure, that despite my conventional upbringing

206 THE HOUSE WITH THE BROKEN TWO

and the strange silences that often incapacitated my voice, I had always had the inclination to question the unquestionable.

That day, I realized that the feminist version of me hadn't come out of what I had learned in university. It was born on a dark spring night back in 1968 when I gave birth to my first child alone in a big crowded hospital. I knew at last that my feminism stems from the invisibility society demanded for unwed mothers back then; I knew that my sense of agency was born in a social order that dictated no one should stop to comfort a frightened eighteen-year-old girl in labour simply because she wasn't married.

After the excitement of reuniting with my son settled down, I turned my attention back to my dissertation, but I found that I had no heart for it anymore. It sounded ever so proper and serious, even dry and fruitless. I couldn't write those kinds of sentences any longer and wanted release from the academic voice. I had changed, and I couldn't hide that. I wanted to show that dissertations come out of people who aren't cerebral robots, but living beings whose work is always affected by who they are, where they have come from, and what's happening in their personal lives.

On that snowy October afternoon after I had mailed a letter to the son I thought I would never see again, I knew for the first time that being a feminist and being a mother are inevitably connected, like fetus and placenta. I knew that day that I had to investigate those intimate antagonists: feminism and motherhood. I knew that I had to put myself into whatever I wrote. But I didn't want to discard everything I had already written. I began to devise a method in which I could develop my new ideas and still retain some of the work I had completed before my son came back into my life. As a differently shaped dissertation came together in my mind, I started to feel excited about it again.

Unfortunately, I discovered that my project supervisor had no enthusiasm for—or even mild interest in—my new direction. I persevered and asked for a meeting so I could present my proposed changes to my whole committee. The day before that meeting, my supervisor abruptly resigned from my project. In the following tumultuous weeks, I had to negotiate the numerous hurdles academic faculty members can use to cause havoc in their graduate students' lives. Fortunately, just as I thought an oncoming train was about to flatten me, I found a new supervisor, one who was supportive, even enthusiastic, about what I wanted to do with my project.

With my new supervisor's guidance and advocacy, I finally completed and defended my dissertation. At long last, I heard my name called out and walked across the convocation stage wearing a black doctoral robe trimmed with blue and gold velvet, my husband and children sitting in the audience cheering me on. I felt pleased that all those years of wanting to go to university had come to an end with me going as far as I could go. Yet, when I look back on my time as a Ph.D. student, I can only describe it as a strange, somewhat disappointing experience. Sometimes I wonder why I wanted it so much.

Before I graduated, I had expected to come through my university years brimming with energy and confidence. All through my studies, I definitely planned to use my Ph.D. to develop an academic career, even at my age. But, with three degrees finally hanging on my wall at home, I felt no energetic elation, no calm confidence. Instead, I was physically run-down and emotionally demoralized. Moreover, I was no longer drawn to the intellectual mystique of the academic world. I had lost my naive belief that being part of the humanities academy would be a kinder, indeed more humane, work environment than others I had experienced in my life. My years of working and studying in a busy university department had shown me that academia is as prone to posturing, deceit, and betrayal as any other workplace, perhaps even more so.

Nevertheless, the first time a student called me "Dr. Coulter," I felt great satisfaction. I continued to teach English and writing for a while, working as a contract or "sessional" instructor. For a few years, I thought I could be content with that kind of work, renewing my teaching commitment from one year to the next. But it soon proved to be less than satisfying. After eight years of teaching first-year English, I realized that I had had enough. Each year more and more students seemed to come out of high school with a greater sense of entitlement, with a greater disdain for language and good writing skills, with an indignant demand that they receive high grades for poor quality work. Whereas I used to stand in front of a classroom and feel my energy rise as I connected with my students, I found myself standing up there with little or no energy at all. It was time for me to leave teaching behind. Now I spend my working days writing. I think I'm becoming a storyteller.

One of my favourite stories is about having all four of my children present in my life today. After years of keeping my oldest son's existence a secret, I never tire of saying his name out loud, especially in the same sentence with mine. Since our reunion, I have told our story many times. Sometimes it's an abbreviated version; sometimes my audience asks for more. Every time I tell it, whether at a lunch with friends or a happy-hour gathering or a dinner party, after I've finished, someone always says "Something like that happened in my family" or "I think I have a cousin/niece/nephew I've never met" or "I remember when my best friend had to go into a home for unwed mothers." Occasionally, a woman around my age will pull me aside later and whisper in my ear: "I have one, too." Even a few men have confided that they have a missing child out in the world somewhere.

I've learned to hear these other stories without saying much, making sure that whoever is speaking knows I'm listening carefully to what they say. I do my best to maintain a calm exterior because I don't want to let any feelings I have disturb the tentative hold I know they have on their emotions. I store their experiences inside me, beside my own, and marvel at the healing that happens simply by giving voice to an untold story, telling it out loud to a listening audience.

I have also been gathering stories about my more distant family history. I collect information in several file folders, thinking that some day I will write about one or two of my ancestors: perhaps my Icelandic great-grandmother's voyage from Iceland across the Atlantic to Canada, or those two great-great-grandfathers who came from Scotland to build their lives in what would become Manitoba. I have started doing research in archives and libraries because, other than my siblings and my cousins, the only living information source left in my family from the previous generation is my mother.

Unfortunately, as she moves into her elder years, my mother's reluctance to talk about the past has been superseded by a physical inability to speak. I think it was on her seventy-fifth birthday that I noticed something was happening to my mother. She still looked good, younger than her years. She had remarried and seemed happy in her life with her new husband. On that summer day, we gathered together to celebrate the many August birthdays in our family. We all worked together in my sister's kitchen preparing a big buffet dinner. One of the recipes must have called for almonds. My mother tried to use the word in a sentence, but couldn't think of it and stopped for a long moment. One of us prompted her: "Almonds, Mom." She tried to repeat it, but said "Ay-mand" instead. I remember correcting her. I remember that it happened several times that afternoon. I remember that she laughed at herself each time.

Over the next few years, my mother aged rapidly. Each time I saw her, I noticed that she was getting smaller, shrinking in size. She was always a strong, sturdy woman. There was a time when I felt as if she towered over me. Now I looked down to make eye contact with her, and instead of reaching up to hug her, my arm settled low around her shoulders. By this time, my sisters and I had realized that something was definitely happening to her ability to speak. Her vocabulary was shrinking along with her body. She often struggled to find the right words for what she wanted to say.

She started to use the word *thing* a lot: "I can't find that thing ...you know ... that thing ... for eggs?" *Do you mean a whisk, Mom?* "Yes," she would say, relief evident in her voice, "a whisk. I don't

know why I can't think of the . . . things . . ." When we had that
conversation, I remember thinking that it was odd she was even
looking for a whisk because she didn't cook much anymore. She
didn't make meals or bake cakes anymore. She didn't make gravy
anymore. Indeed, she didn't do much of anything anymore.

Initially diagnosed as a type of aphasia, my mother's condition
is now advanced dementia. Her problems in finding specific words
gradually developed into difficulties in forming sentences.
Eventually she struggled to make herself understood at all. She
forgot almost all nouns and rarely used an active verb. Her
vocabulary consisted mostly of interjections and pronouns: *you
know, here, this, her, the one over there.* Strangely, she still knew
numbers well, but only up to ten. When she turned eighty, she
said she was "Eight-oh."

In a sense, she is already lost to us. I know that it is no longer
possible to ask her questions about family history, no longer
possible to ask her anything about herself or my father, no longer
possible to hope that some day she might eventually reveal
whatever it was she almost told me that day after our year-long
estrangement.

As her dementia progressed, I noticed that, in many ways,
my aging mother had become childlike; she smiled a lot, but also
looked puzzled much of the time. Ironically, she was suddenly
chatty. The woman who so often used silence as a punishment
now wanted to talk a lot, but much of the time no one could
understand what she was saying. Conversations with her were
short and disjointed. When I talked to her on the phone last
spring, we were several minutes into our chat when she inter-

rupted what I was saying. Forming the first complete sentence I had heard her make in several months, she asked me a question: "What is your name?"

I didn't know then that, a few short months later, she wouldn't be able to say her own name, let alone mine; that her conversation would be reduced to the fillers that she has used all her life, phrases such as "Boy oh boy" or "Isn't that something" or "And how!" I once thought that nothing could be as devastating as my father's sudden death. I was wrong. It has been equally traumatic and heartbreaking to watch my mother's slow disintegration. Throughout my life, my feelings about my parents have always made me uneasy because I thought I loved my father more than I loved my mother. I know now that's not true.

On a happier note, an unexpected bonus has come out of having my son back in my life. When I left Winnipeg back in 1970, I never wanted to return. In fact, if possible, I avoided going back to the city of my birth or anywhere in my home province unless absolutely necessary. Now, I have my hometown back in my life as well as my son. I visit Winnipeg a couple of times each year. I am surprised at how good it feels to walk through familiar city streets again, to take my grandson to Assiniboine Park, to have brunch at the old Pancake House on Pembina Highway, to drive out to see the Christmas light display near Assiniboia Downs. I have even gone back up to Lake Winnipeg, walked around Gimli and Winnipeg Beach, strolled out onto the pier beside my uncle's Ponemah "castle," still recognizable to me. Only once have I sauntered past our old house. The two was still broken.

Last spring, my old high school held another big reunion. I spent four days in Winnipeg visiting my son and his family. I also attended several reunion events, running into former classmates I hadn't seen for years. Over that weekend, I told many of them about my first pregnancy and reuniting with my son. They listened well, reacted to my story with warmth and understanding. I felt no negative judgment from them at all. I felt at home.

ABOUT THE AUTHOR

Myrl Coulter was born in Winnipeg, Manitoba. She has a Ph.D. from the University of Alberta where she taught in the Department of English and Film Studies for eight years. She won a 1995 National Screen Institute Drama Prize for her short screenplay *Willpower*. In previous careers, Myrl has been a cashier, a bank clerk, an x-ray technician, a stay-at-home mom, a receptionist, a sales representative, a small business owner, and a stills photographer in the film industry. She has been a writer all her life. Myrl lives in Edmonton, Alberta.

A NOTE ON THE
FIRST BOOK COMPETITION

The national First Book Competition, sponsored by The Writer's Studio at Simon Fraser University to celebrate its 10th anniversary, was a first in Canada. It was a response to the ever increasing difficulty new or emerging writers face in trying to get their work published. Contest organizers received 200+ submissions, coming from Canadian writers as far away as Italy and New Zealand.

Partnering publisher, Anvil Press, agreed to publish the three winning entries in the genres of creative non-fiction, fiction, and poetry.

The three First Book Competition winners are all Canadian writers, writing in English, who have not previously published a book. They submitted original, book-length manuscripts to the competition.

The winners are: Myrl Coulter of Edmonton, Alberta for *The House with the Broken Two* (Creative Nonfiction), Jackie Bateman of Vancouver for *Nondescript Rambunctious* (Fiction), and Rachel Thompson of Vancouver for *Galaxy* (Poetry).

The Writer's Studio is a one-year, continuing studies creative writing certificate program at Simon Fraser University. For more information visit: www.thewritersstudio.ca.